PRAISE FOR *W...*

Ayres has achieved the extraordinary. In choosing to write about
the beauty of music, and life itself, he has created something
gorgeous in its own right. This book has an almost divine presence
that reaches into the reader. I am not a musician, or even remotely
talented in the field, but in this work I felt exposed to the sublime
majesty of it all through Ayres' talent, vulnerability and humour.
This is a precious book, overwhelming in its sensory evocations
and more necessary than ever in the current moment.
Rick Morton, author

With deceptively simple prose, Ed offers a truly beguiling
account of himself, intertwined with the miracle that undergirds
everything – the music that saved his life. The clarity
on display in his writing is memorable.
Geraldine Doogue, broadcaster

PRAISE FOR *CADENCE*

[Ayres'] passion for music is never far from the surface.
Nick Galvin, *Sydney Morning Herald*

provocative, intelligent, surprising and funny ...
Australian Arts Review

PRAISE FOR *DANGER MUSIC*

Ayres writes with forthrightness and compassion in
this timely, powerfully told tale.
Fiona Capp, *Sydney Morning Herald*

Ed Ayres is a writer, musician and broadcaster. He was born on the White Cliffs of Dover and began playing music when he was six years old. He studied music in Manchester, Berlin and London, played professionally in the UK and Hong Kong and moved to Australia in 2003. Ed is the presenter of ABC Classic's *Weekend Breakfast*.

Ed has written three other books: *Cadence*, about his journey by bicycle from England to Hong Kong with only a violin for company; *Danger Music*, describing his year teaching music in Afghanistan; and *Sonam and the Silence*, a children's book about the importance of music. Ed's books have been shortlisted for several prestigious awards, including the Prime Minister's Literary Awards.

Ed was born Emma and transitioned just before his fiftieth birthday. Better late than never.

WHOLE NOTES

WHOLE
NOTES

WHOLE NOTES

Life Lessons
Through Music

ED
AYRES

ABC
BOOKS

The ABC 'Wave' device is a trademark of the
Australian Broadcasting Corporation and is used
under licence by HarperCollins*Publishers* Australia.

HarperCollins*Publishers*
Australia • Brazil • Canada • France • Germany • Holland • Hungary
India • Italy • Japan • Mexico • New Zealand • Poland • Spain • Sweden
Switzerland • United Kingdom • United States of America

First published in Australia in 2021
by HarperCollins*Publishers* Australia Pty Limited
Level 13, 201 Elizabeth Street, Sydney NSW 2000
ABN 36 009 913 517
harpercollins.com.au

A catalogue record for this book is available from the National Library of Australia.

ISBN 978 0 7333 4103 8 (paperback)
ISBN 978 1 4607 1279 5 (ebook)

Cover design by Andy Warren, HarperCollins Design Studio
Cover image by Pixel Stories/Stocksy.com/2539059
Internal illustrations by Andy Warren, HarperCollins Design Studio
Author photograph by Greville Patterson
Typeset in Minion Pro by Kelli Lonergan
Printed and bound in Australia by McPherson's Printing Group

for Charlie –
my lioness, my sun

CONTENTS

And you? When will you
begin that long journey
into yourself?

RUMI

_____

PRELUDE

THIS IS THE MOMENT, before the music begins. A moment of deepest silence – between breath, between thought, between sound itself.

The musician, instrument in hand, walks on stage and takes their bow.

They bow to you, for coming to listen.

They bow to themselves, for their dedication to their art.

They bow to the musicians who have come before them and kept this art alive.

But above all, they bow to music itself.

This ritual is at the birth of every concert, no matter the skill of the performer, the age of the performer, the type of music or where the music is played. This ritual is our step into beauty.

Because music consoles and restores us. Through music, whether we are listening or playing, we know ourselves more intimately, more honestly, and more clearly with every note. And with every note, music offers us a hand to the beyond.

Through music, we can say what we didn't even know we felt.

This book is an ode to music, and a celebration of humanity's greatest creation. And this book is not a call to arms but a call to instruments.

Music offers us gifts we can open every day to make our lives whole, so let the playing begin.

A:
BRAVERY

This will be our reply to violence: to make music more intensely, more beautifully, more devotedly than ever before.

LEONARD BERNSTEIN

THIS AFTERNOON AT THREE, something important is going to happen. A young girl is going to have her first music lesson.

The teacher in charge of this huge moment is profoundly nervous. I know, because I am that teacher. I have been teaching music for thirty years, but no matter how many lessons I give, I am always nervous before a first lesson, because it is the first lesson the student remembers most. This lesson will set the colour and mood of their music learning, possibly for years to come.

So I'd better not stuff it up.

I've heard from Rosie's mum that Rosie is beyond excited. She has her cello, a notebook, her music book and an enthusiasm that will not fit in a cello case, or any case, for that matter. Rosie has been declaring for a while that she wants to play the cello, and now she is ready. Rosie has already shown bravery, commitment and patience.

You might ask, why am I nervous? After all, it's only music, it's only a first lesson, Rosie is only seven, and only and only and only.

Well, I suppose I'm nervous because this isn't *only* a first lesson in music. I believe that learning music, more than any other field, helps us to truly understand ourselves.

Over the months and, I hope, years to come, Rosie's learning is going to be led by the first sense to come in our lives, and the last sense to leave our lives – hearing. She is going to learn that hearing is different from listening. She is going to learn that our bodies and minds are one, and what we think we can do is what we end up being able to do.

She is going to learn persistence. She is going to learn that tiny steps, taken each day, create a journey unimaginable in length and adventure. She is going to learn that it is alright not to be able to do something. But then, note by note, she will succeed.

She is going to learn to express emotions rather than keep them inside where they can twist and warp us.

She is going to learn the kindness of music, especially when we play music with and for others.

She is going to learn just how much you can do, even when you are seven years old.

Rosie is going to learn not only how to learn but why we learn.

And Rosie is going to learn that music will always be there. She will learn that from today, until the end of her life, she will never be alone. Because at some point in her life, Rosie is going to have best friends leave and family members die, have her faith disappointed and find life hopeless and overwhelming.

And in those moments, when Rosie thinks back to these lessons in music, she will realise they were really lessons in living.

—————————————————

Five years ago, I was reborn. And I was reborn through music.

I was born in a female body, given the sex marker of female, named Emma, and taken through the usual rituals of a girl's life. And, since I was born in the late sixties when knowledge of transgender issues was barely in its infancy, I lived my life as it was laid out for me.

As a female.

I was told to put on a t-shirt around ten years old and from then on, nothing seemed to fit me, neither clothes, feelings, my mind nor my body. The only thing that did fit was music.

Mrs Turner, the music teacher at our primary school in Shrewsbury, was my first music prophet. Her perfect plump body was perpetually wrapped in a brown woollen dress, blossoming into a floral one in the tenuous summers of the 1970s. Mrs Turner had kind hands and made *Ring a Ring o' Rosie* on the piano sound like a Schubert song cycle. She believed every child should have the gift of music, and boy was she committed. Over a term of lunchtimes, in the English drizzle by the swings, Mrs Turner harangued my mates and me until we came to her recorder class. Once there, she grabbed our tiny six-year-old hands, scrawled the note names E, G, B, D and F on our right fingers, and F, A, C, E on the palm between. A plastic recorder was stuffed into the other hand, a sheet of what looked like hieroglyphics laid in front of us and off we went.

Did anyone say shrill? Everyone at some point in their life, especially if they have an ear or artery that needs unblocking, should experience a classroom full of tiny children playing plastic recorders. Those little bodies were all lung and bellow. Their noise brought a certain clarity to life and the class brought a certain clarity to my brain, because through Mrs Turner and her music lessons I began to develop an inner imagination, an inner structure and a magnificent inner world: I began to think in music. Those lunchtime classes were my passport to the Promised Land and Mrs Turner was my Moses.

After a year or so of plastic shrillness I could read music without looking at the letter names on my fingers and I felt it was time to move up in the world. Playing recorder was for infants, and I was eight. You can do a lot when you're eight. I could certainly decide which instrument I wanted to play.

Throughout our lives, we are faced with decisions that define us. Defining us in not only how we see ourselves but in how others see us. The decisions sneak into our lives, sometimes made with hardly a thought, like whether to drink whisky or gin, or which sport to play, or if red really does go with pink.

Tiny decisions no-one but you really care about, but these small decisions make us the characters we are; they are the little puffs of wind that take us across the ocean. In our lives, most of us do not have to make life or death decisions, and so we don't take much notice of these seemingly inconsequential choices, but they add up. They do matter. Every note matters.

I believe one of those decisions is which instrument we choose to play. Or, indeed, whether we can choose to play one at all. Or maybe we never have the chance to decide and the decision was made for us when we were children and our parents took an inexplicable, gendered view: cello is for boys, violin is for girls.

I stumbled into this gender morass after receiving my first musical benediction, Jacqueline du Pré, the English cellist from the 1960s, playing Maria Theresa von Paradis' *Sicilienne*. Even though it was on a tiny record player with a speaker the size of a teacup, Jacqueline's sound, as she balanced the soft doubt of the melody with the glee of the dance rhythm, her sound, her sound, her sound seemed to explain everything in my young heart. I was never christened or baptised or given any religious encouragement as a child (one time, when I wanted to go to church as a ten-year-old, Mum sighed. 'Oh, if you must …'), but this moment satisfied everything I needed. There are some performers who are so completely and utterly compelling with their instruments that you feel, watching and listening to them, they are connected to a higher world. Jacqueline du Pré was that person for me.

I asked my mum if I could play the cello. It seemed I could not, should not, since cello was for boys and I was called Emma. I had been born in a body that was very clearly female, and that body, never mind my mind, could play violin, thank you very much, as the violin, in 1975, was for girls.

And that was that.

If Mrs Turner was my music prophet, I now needed some more down-to-earth inspiration. Mrs Llewellyn, bent over and a little frayed around the edges, was the local violin teacher. It looked like the high notes of the violin had damaged her inner and outer spirit, but she persevered, week by week, her lessons efficient, strict and slightly dull.

But dull lessons didn't matter, because I had had an epiphany. As I went through primary school, I realised that even though my family was poor and my parents were divorced and we didn't have a car and my best friend was about to leave because her mum had died, despite all of that, I had a superpower: I could look at little black dots written on five lines hundreds of years ago and I could make them into sound, sound that could make people cry, or clap, or laugh. And even if no-one listened to me, I could be on my own for hours on end and I could play my instrument and not be bothered by vicious family rows or my sister running away again.

I was a magician.

I was a time traveller.

I lived in a different universe.

I had music.

Musicians hone our playing for nearly all our lives. We may begin with the instrument our parents want us to play, but eventually we become the musicians *we* want to be. We do this by working alone and with other musicians, slowly finding and developing the best way to reveal the truth of our art. And we do that by listening to ourselves.

From the beginning of our life to its end, unless we are born or become deaf, the sense of hearing accompanies us. It is our first sense to develop and the last to leave. As babies, we develop our hearing in the womb. You remember those young recorder players? One of the first notes we learn on the recorder is the first pitch we respond to in the womb, B, nearly an octave above middle C. Yes, that B, one finger and the thumb behind. As we grow in the womb, our hearing ability spreads slowly downwards and upwards, until we can hear the low open G string of a cello and a piercing whistle. Our hearing also becomes more acute as the sounds we hear become quieter and quieter. From the recorder down to the cello and up beyond a high soprano, inside the womb we are experiencing sound in the most intense way we may ever experience it. No wonder those recorders are so welcome when we finally play them.

This coming into the world through sound is repeated every day as we wake. And as we fall through our lives towards death, the reverse happens: our hearing becomes limited, the people on the radio always seem to mumble, and yet, even in a coma and near death, we can still hear.

When my mother was nearly eighty-five, she had a severe stroke in her cerebellum. The doctors at the specialist stroke unit were exquisitely compassionate but still predicted only a fifty-fifty chance of survival. They gave Mum a drug to bring down the swelling in her brain; it didn't work, so they gave her some more. Beyond the recommended dose, they admitted, but Mum had been unconscious for over a week. I flew from Australia to England to see her, as I believed then, before she died, and the person who lay before me in the bed was a theatrical simulacrum of my mother. Her mouth twisted in a grimace, her massive hands lay limp and bruised, her eyes squeezed tightly shut. I am a musician, so I did what a musician would do: I played Mum some music.

I had prepared some playlists on my phone, and I put on the Chopin Nocturne in E-flat major. I wetted Mum's lips with a little water, smoothed her hair and together we had the simplest of bonds: we listened.

It was something we had done countless times before. We used to listen to concerts together, to LPs, to the proms on the telly or visiting soloists in the relative backwater of Shropshire. And now we listened to this music that Chopin composed when he was twenty, music written not far off two hundred years ago. The piece has such a gentle tread, a melody that goes around in a circle of sad delight. In one hand the music lifts you onto a safe escarpment of youthful love, and with the other hand the harmonies take you into the shadows of life, a reminder that as much as perfection can exist, only the slightest change of perception will alter the mood and direction of your life.

As Mum listened, suddenly her eyes opened and she gazed directly at me, almost through me. In that moment, I realised together we had experienced human beauty at its most powerful. And only music could have melded us together in such a traumatic time, with this my first visit since changing from Mum's third 'daughter' to her second son. It was all forgotten, it was all so completely unimportant, because we had opened our hearts to music and, through that, to each other.

As the days went on, Mum would drift in and out of consciousness. She still had swelling on her brain, and as she started to speak, I wondered whether Mum had had a stroke or the stroke had had her. Her always vivid blue eyes were now milky, her mouth formed chaotically around once clear words. Who knew what strange reality had raged or trundled through her brain during that lost time? Who knew what the music was doing to her mind? Was she back in the womb, hearing a shrill B on the recorder? The weeks went by and Mum was moved to a long-term stroke ward, filled with drooling young men and devastated wives. Mum started to speak ... in French. I swapped from Chopin and Mozart to some Debussy, a little bit of fun Poulenc, and gradually Mum's eyes cleared, every day a new blue. Her mouth, often grim from a tough life of divorce and some tricky children, had now softened into something unbearably surprising. A smile. A tender, cheeky smile. Mum was coming back. And she had travelled back to me on the magic carpet of music. Mum had listened, even with a swollen, comatose brain.

We hear beyond consciousness. Western scientists have investigated the sense of sound and how it survives even when we are close to death, and their discovery mirrors Buddhist priests and their practice. A Buddhist priest will advise you to speak only in a positive way around the dying person, and to fill their last hours with kindness and compassionate sounds. So probably no plastic recorders. We continue to hear right up to our death, and the sounds we hear can make a profound difference to the equanimity of our brainwaves and, as Buddhists believe, our path to the first bardo and beyond.

This knowledge of the arc of listening, of how listening envelopes our lives, this knowledge changes listening from a passive receiving of shallow information to something much deeper, something more essential. Our hearing is the swaddling and the shroud of our lives.

Through learning music, we train ourselves to listen. Properly listen. And when we train ourselves to listen through music, our sense of hearing becomes exceptional. With our hearing we can discern the tiniest change in pitch, tone and direction. I know because I witness it in every lesson with my students.

The afternoon has arrived for Rosie's first cello lesson. I go over my notes and remind myself of the things I would like to leave behind: happiness and comfort and the seeds of joy in music.

I arrive at the appointed hour and am met by a laughing young girl. Rosie can barely contain herself and jigs and jives on her chair as we talk.

'Rosie, why did you choose the cello?'

'I love the sound it makes!' And with her arms, Rosie imitates a bird soaring into the clouds.

We take her small cello from its case, lay it carefully on its side and stand to bow. I explain I am bowing to thank her for being my student as I will learn as much from her as she will from me. And she is bowing to me for teaching her but also bowing to the musicians who have gone before us and kept our music safe.

As a teacher, the ritual of the bow at the beginning and end of every lesson offers many gifts. The bow gives a clear indication the lesson has started and finished. The bow shows the teacher the ability of the student to copy, and their broad ability to control their body. How the student responds to the bow gives an idea of their mood in that moment. The bow reminds me, the teacher, of my responsibility to this student, and her unique path with the cello. And finally, to make a bow with integrity, the student and the teacher need to show humility, and that is a sign of courage.

We bow in as many ways as a child and a middle-aged chap can dream up, and then we sit and look at our beautiful instruments, our cellos.

Teachers need to think about the harvest in years to come to understand what to plant in the first lesson, and one of those crucial elements is being able to care for an instrument. Even though Rosie's cello is a basic rented student model, she may eventually play on one worth thousands of dollars, so Rosie needs to learn how to take care of her cello as if it's a baby: no leaving it in the car, no leaving it on the floor, no sitting on it, no dropping it, no using it as a cricket bat (yes, I have seen that), no letting it get dirty, no abandoning it. Make sure it is loved by playing it every day. Our instrument is our best friend.

Cellists will spend tens of thousands of hours in our lives sitting and playing the cello, so learning how to sit well is crucial. We sit at the front of our chairs and at the back, we stand as quickly as we can with feet together and as quickly as we can with feet apart, we slouch and sit up straight, we sit with our feet off the floor and firmly down like a tree – all this to find out for ourselves where the best place is for everything.

As Rosie sits with her cello resting against her heart, I ask her to listen as I tap on the cello's different parts. I tell her their names – scroll, neck, shoulders, ribs, belly and back – then ask her to close her eyes and listen. I tap again and, as Rosie's listening focuses, she names each part without faltering. Her hearing, her listening, is awakening.

After bowing and baby-caring and sitting and listening,

Rosie is truly ready to make music. I show her how to pluck her four strings and we try copycat – I play, Rosie copies. Different rhythms, different strings, all ever so slowly increasing in complexity.

And finally, for this first lesson, Rosie's first cello song. Plucked and sung to the four strings, C, G, D and A – Cats Get Dogs Angry going up, Angry Dogs Get Cats going down (depending on whether you're a cat or dog person).

I love my cello.
It is not yellow,
But it sounds mellow.
I love my cello!

Because Rosie's listening has been awakened by the tapping, when she copies my playing it is joyous and confident. Because the tapping is awakened by Rosie sitting well, it is joyous and confident. Because the sitting well is awakened by the baby-caring, it is joyous and confident. Because the baby-caring is awakened by the bow, it is joyous and confident. And because her bow is awakened by her brave choice to play the cello, it is joyous and confident.

We have started the lesson with a bow, and now, to show our respect for music and its gifts, we end the lesson with a bow. Rosie has created a virtuous circle.

And the first step is the bravest. Rosie has chosen to be a musician.

While I was thinking about this book and how I really want it to be an inspiration for people of all ages to start or restart an instrument, I thought I should probably start an instrument myself, to remind myself of the glories of learning something new. Okay, and to remind myself of how bloody hard it is and how dreadful it can sound and how you don't really want to practise, you want to share a bottle of red wine instead and watch *The Crown*, but you still haven't done your bloody scales and you can't play the piece your teacher gave you, which you heard a seven-year-old play fluently in the lesson before you. Sound familiar?

Since I am a musician (well, I spent six years at music college so I'm making a good go of it), I figured I should give myself something really, really challenging, an instrument I know absolutely nothing about, an instrument with a reputation for being one of the hardest. All this to simulate the experience of a non-musician playing something easy to get your hands around, like a recorder.

The oboe and the horn have the reputation of being the hardest instruments. No offence to oboists, I love your instrument, but I don't really fancy spending hours whittling bamboo to make reeds, so I choose the horn. I've wanted to have a go for years, and now I have a reason. Or an excuse. I can't decide which.

I break the news to my partner, Charlie. Although this is a chapter about bravery, I am a total coward and take days to find the right way to tell my beloved I am going to be playing a very, very loud instrument at home for at least an hour a day.

Just like walking on stage for a solo gig, I take the plunge.

'Gorgeous, you know I'm writing a book about the lessons of music?'

'Yes.'

'And you know I want it to inspire people to take up instruments?'

'Yes …' (A note of worry coming in now. See, listening helps in relationships too. Who knew?)

'Well, I've decided I need to start a new instrument.'

At this Charlie puts down her book and looks up, her beautiful eyes waiting patiently for the hammer blow.

'Yes?'

'And it's the horn. The French horn.' I feel a need to clarify the curly French horn rather than the lesser-known Saxhorn that's very hard to find a teacher for, let alone an actual instrument.

'Okay.'

'Really? Is that it? Just … okay? I thought you'd have something a bit more, um, lively to say about it.'

Charlie is a deeply spiritual person who spent six years studying Buddhism and Sufism in Indonesia. She has spent her life developing calmness, a calmness that is now tested to its limits.

The calmness holds. I am even more in love with her.

'If you need to do that to write a good book, horn away. Who's going to teach you?'

Hmm. That is a good question.

I decide to do some deep research, which means typing the words 'horn teacher Queensland Conservatorium' into Google. I find an associate professor called Peter Luff, who is head of performance. Well, I've heard of him so he must be pretty good, I think blithely. I write him an email.

Dear Peter,

I had a chat a while ago with a couple of your students from the Con. I have been wanting to play the horn for years, and they said you are an excellent teacher!

Do you have any space? I played the viola professionally so can read simple music. Well, the alto clef. And a lot of rests.

I do not understand transposition in any way. Why do you guys have to do that?

Let me know! I'm super keen!

Thanks,

Ed

In my defence, I use a lot of exclamation marks when I'm nervous. Or just excited.

Peter's reply came just a few hours later.

Dear Ed,

I would be only too happy to teach you the horn, and I promise transposition doesn't come along until lesson two.

Let me know when you'd like to start and please feel free to contact me on my mobile if you like.

All the best,

Peter

Ooh, I'm liking this already. I've thrown in a casual joke about one of the hardest things about music, which is that sometimes musicians, in their head as they're playing, need to change the notes written on the page. This is called transposition, and it comes on top of the horn already being a transposing instrument by default. Some instruments, when they have a written C, *what actually comes out of the instrument is an F*. It's called 'horn in F'. But why? It's all to do with different sizes (therefore different pitches) of instruments from hundreds of years ago, and this is the size people liked the best, so it stuck. The horn, along with trumpet, clarinet and saxophone, is therefore called a transposing instrument. But wait there's more. A horn player might play a written C that comes out as an F, but sometimes the composer writes a C but wants it to come out as an E flat, if they are writing for a different size horn. The horn player then needs to do this extra transposition in their head. For a transposing chap like me, the horn is a good choice but mental transposition is way, way down the list of things to learn. Still, Peter has returned serve with my joke so I reckon I'm onto a good thing.

We arrange to meet at his house the following week. All I need to bring, apparently, are my lips and lungs. Peter, being a horn player, has a spare one. Horn, that is.

At this point I should probably tell you a bit more about the horn. First up, it's not called the French horn anymore, and only ever was by the Dutch and English, because the French made some excellent hunting horns back in the 1600s or so – crikey, talk about brand stickiness. If we wanted to give a nationality to it we should probably call the horn the German horn, as the Germans were the first to develop a clever way to change the length of the horn, and therefore the different notes available, by swapping the parts of the horn called crooks. I can feel you being pulled into this wonderfully arcane world already. By hook or by crook.

The horn is one of the very oldest instruments. In its original form – that is, ripped from an animal's head, likely a ram, and then blown into (easier to do when the ram isn't attached) – the horn was and still is used for some religious ceremonies, particularly in Judaism. During the Bronze Age, Greece, Iceland and several countries in Scandinavia developed a horn-like instrument called the lur, made from bronze and later wood, sometimes two metres long, which they used to frighten their enemies or to herd cattle. Possibly at the same time if you didn't like cows.

Horns used for hunting back in the fourteenth century were made from some questionable materials – boiled leather horn, anyone? Thankfully, the French started to experiment with brass alloys to make conical tubes. They also wrapped the tube into a handy coil to sling over your shoulder while cantering on your horse, who hopefully liked the feeling of a very loud instrument being blown backwards onto their bottom. The coil, like the name, stuck. Except for alphorns, which remain uncoiled. At least you can use them as skis if you get into trouble on the pistes. And the coiled horn is easier to carry on the bus.

And so the journey of the horn began. There are different versions of the horn all around the world, much like the violin or drums. We blow our own horn everywhere, it seems.

Another reason I love the idea of playing the horn is that, traditionally, the horn tells you what to do and where to go. Ah, the sledgehammer of metaphor.

The horn has a reputation as a fearsomely difficult instrument. I'll go into this a little later, but basically, with your lips you are playing in stilettos on a tightrope above a crocodile-infested river hundreds of metres below. Just one wrong thought and you're a goner. It's a wonder anyone even begins to play, knowing the journey ahead. Hmm. Maybe that's why people usually start at foolhardy puberty rather than staid fifty-three. Then again, I have just gone through male puberty (and menopause at the same time), so perhaps it won't be too bad.

Peter is waiting for me outside his house. For a man who has spent much of his life mastering the hardest instrument in the world, he looks surprisingly relaxed. Twinkly, even.

I step into his teaching room and see a piece of my new world before me – shiny, with a lot of bendy bits.

Peter is delightful. I explain I am learning the horn not only because I've always wanted to but also to write a book, and he is up for anything. Although underneath the twinkles I see a seriousness and dedication to the instrument, which is why he has been so successful: associate principal horn in the Queensland Symphony Orchestra, regular principal player with many of the big orchestras in Australia, one of the finest players and teachers in the country and a very well-regarded conductor to boot. Asking Peter to teach me is a bit like asking Warren Buffett to look after my piggy bank money. I'm a tad concerned I might be wasting his time. Crikey, I'd better practise a lot.

Peter picks up the horn he is lending me and immediately pulls a bit off the end. Oh god, he's broken it! Then I see it's the mouthpiece, the bit you can change to suit your own lip shape. He assesses my lips and teeth (British, but not too much) and says I have the perfect mouth for the horn, not too big, not too small. I never realised I was so close to failure right at the start.

'Okay, put your little finger in your mouth, just the end, and suck on it.'

I feel I am being initiated into some strange cult.

'Now imagine you're spitting a seed out of your mouth.'

This is not what I had in mind when I decided to play the most magnificent instrument of them all. I do it anyway and spit out a little bit of … spit. Embarrassing.

'Good!'

Peter goes on to explain about the muscles we (well, I *am* a horn player now) use to create an embouchure, or lip shape. The sucking muscles are the first we develop as babies, and they are the ones that keep the corners of the mouth firm. You can try it now: stick the end of your little finger in your mouth and suck. There you go. Now you're a horn player too.

I feel it's time to celebrate and have a beer, but instead of a beer bottle on my lips, Peter demonstrates how to place the mouthpiece on the embouchure, a third on the lower lip and two thirds above.

'Now take a deep breath into your belly and deflate into the mouthpiece.'

I get wound up for my big moment, making my first sound on the horn. Well, a bit of the end of the horn.

I suck my finger. I spit out the seed. I place the mouthpiece carefully, one third down, two thirds up. I breathe into my belly and think I really need to lose some weight. I deflate and, miracle of miracles, a weak buzz comes from my lips.

'Good! You're a natural!'

My lips tickle and I wonder if that is how Botox feels.

We do it again, and again, and a few more agains, until Peter is satisfied I am sucking and firming and positioning and deflating correctly. Then he asks me to pick up the rest of the horn.

I pick it up gingerly and immediately bash it into the music stand. Whoops. The viola doesn't have a sticky-out bell. Peter explains some of the curly bits and valves, puts the mouthpiece on the horn and we go through the same process.

I put the horn to my lips, or, should I say, my embouchure.

The absolute main reason I want to play the horn is because of its sound. Most of the great composers have used the horn's sound, either as a solo or the four-horn section, to create moments of bliss inside the orchestra. In the right hands, or lips, it is the sound of kindness, calmness and heroism. The horn is bravery in sound, in practice, in effort, in every way.

I breathe in, thinking of the great horn moments in music – Strauss's *A Hero's Life*, Tchaikovsky's Symphony No. 5, Rachmaninoff's Piano Concerto No. 2 – and I prepare to join the pantheon of horny glory makers.

And I breathe out.

It can only be described as a feeble moan. I produce the sound of a small elephant that has hurt its trunk and cannot find its mother. The noise is not calm, it is not kind, and it is not even close to being heroic.

My spirit deflates along with my lungs. This is going to be a long road.

But I take a deep breath and have another go.

I have stepped onto the path of horn playing and I couldn't be happier.

One of the great gifts of learning an instrument as an adult is you generally have an idea how the instrument sounds in the hands of an expert. Adult beginners will rarely start the violin if they have never been inspired by its high elegant song, or the trombone if they have never heard it swing. And so, as I go home and start to practise, I try to emulate the horn sound I have been listening to in professional orchestras for decades. My neighbours are delighted about this, especially when I try high notes way beyond my capability. I go for it anyway and listen to Stefan Dohr from the Berlin Philharmonic and Barry Tuckwell, famous Aussie horn player, and trust that just as listening to or reading about a person of high moral character will always inspire us and elevate us, a good-quality sound will do the same.

But what is a good-quality sound?

Now, there's going to be some personal preference here, but generally we may say that Yo-Yo Ma's sound is of a higher quality than mine on the cello, or my eight-year-old student Artie's. Artie makes a promising sound for an eight-year-old, but in Artie's and my sound, there are a few things to develop: richness, smoothness, purity of intonation, sweetness.

Let's look at richness of sound. As we learn to play an instrument, we learn to draw out its resonance through our breath, our bow, or by hitting it (the latter doesn't usually work with a viola, FYI.) Every instrument, including our vocal cords, has an optimum way of vibrating. In practical terms, a rich tone is when the instrument is vibrating as freely as possible.

If the vibrations are free, that means the quality of the sound is complex and deep. And this happens because of a universal law that will blow your mind.

Let us think about a cello string, and the speed at which it is vibrating. The whole length of the string vibrates, and that pitch is called the fundamental note. So far, so easy. If it was only that fundamental note we would be listening to a sine wave, and I don't know how much you listen to them but they are the audio equivalent of unsalted potatoes. So for any sound other than a monotonous sine wave, what is happening is the string is vibrating as a whole but also in infinite divisions of the string. Half the string is vibrating, a third of it, a hundredth of it, and so on ad infinitum. All those different vibrating speeds produce different notes from the fundamental, and because the bits of the string are shorter than the whole, the notes are higher. These notes are called overtones, or the harmonic series, and when we listen to a single note, let's say an A, we can also hear the sound of half the string (double the vibrating speed, so an octave – eight notes – higher A), a third of the string (an octave plus a fifth – five notes – above), a quarter of the string, so another octave, and so on, to a millionth of the string and beyond. Imagine looking at an Egyptian pyramid. The fundamental note is the base, the overtones are the decreasing layers going up and up. When we are listening to a single note we are listening to every note possible and they spiral up, higher and higher, but since we cannot hear as high as a dog can, we only hear the lower notes. Hmm, perhaps my dog, Happy, should be a music critic. Oh wait, she already is. She walks out when I start playing the horn.

What I find so awe-inspiring about the physical fact of overtones is that we have the ability in our fingertips or our lungs to create an entire universe of sound with every single note. And as we develop the ability to re-create the universe, consistently and without ego, we become at one with ourselves and with others. When we create a true note on our instrument it vibrates fully, and we begin to vibrate more fully with it. We teach ourselves, through visceral experience, that every single event in our lives is complex and interconnected. The more we play our instruments with open hearing and heart, the more we recognise the universal beauty in every single sound, and every single being. As we play music, even a single note, we reach deeper and deeper into our awareness and consciousness; we reach beyond time to the eternal here and now. The hear and now.

Many years ago, I had a position playing viola with the English String Orchestra. This was my first job after leaving music college and I loved it. The orchestra is based in Worcester, a small town drenched in English quaintness and probably some sauce as well. Our regular repertoire was, you guessed it, English string music: Elgar, Elgar, bit more Elgar, Walton, Parry, Elgar, Bridge, Elgar and Butterworth. And Elgar. Gentle music that encouraged reasonable acts, like drinking warm beer and saying sorry when someone stepped on your toe. It was a perfect first job made even better by the patron of the orchestra, Lord Yehudi Menuhin. Menuhin was the most famous violinist of his lifetime and there he was, playing a Bach concerto just feet away from me. He had made his name with a recording of the Elgar Concerto, just like Jacqueline du Pré, but on violin this time, not cello, and his sound on that early recording was beyond description. Here was a violinist who transcended what a violin should sound like, to cross over to what it could sound like.

Menuhin's sound imagination knew no bounds, and his musical genres knew no bounds. Menuhin played jazz with Stéphane Grappelli and Indian classical music with Pandit Ravi Shankar, and in these recordings you can hear his open heart and desire to assimilate and learn from those two masters. But it is in his classical recordings that his sound leaps from the speaker. Menuhin had a clarity and honesty to his sound that I don't believe has ever been matched, except perhaps by Hilary Hahn. So when I turned up at the rehearsal for the Bach concerto with Lord Menuhin, I expected this rich, expansive sound, but I had not considered Menuhin's age. At this point he was in his late seventies. No, not old, but he was somewhat frail. As he started to play, the whole orchestra was attentive to every tiny note, and the sound Menuhin now made was completely other. From the lusciousness and plumpness of his youthful sound, his current sound had not hollowed out but somehow distilled. There was nothing extraneous or distracting to conceal the purity of his musical intent; what was left was the line of his playing, the pure shape of his music.

Even though the tone was small and delicate, it moved me beyond any sound, before or since.

Menuhin led an exemplary life. He did not waste his talent; he taught and passed on his knowledge and founded a school in England, he explored other cultures and learnt from them and he founded a music charity, Live Music Now, which continues to bring live music to prisons, schools and hospitals. In his life, and in his sound, Menuhin taught us all the meaning of devotion.

———————————————

It is a Wednesday evening during school term. At a community centre with playing fields in Bardon, nestled under the northwest hills of Brisbane, a jumble of people in the attire of their activity of choice – rugby, football, gymnastics – walk from their parked cars towards the thing they love. But some of the people walk to the centre not dressed in lycra or wicking materials, they do not have studs on their shoes, and they do not have a towel and a ball in their hands. Instead, they are carrying a musical instrument – a cello strapped to their back, a violin or viola swaying gently next to their legs, one tall, elegant woman pushing a double bass on a wheel. The musicians start to gather from 6.30 p.m., and the hall slowly but surely fills as the chairs and music stands are arranged in an arc of attention. It is rehearsal time for the adult beginners' and returning players' orchestra Bardon Strings.

Bardon Strings is unique in Australia. And the woman behind this bravery is Anne Keenan.

Anne began playing violin as a child with a nun called Sister Marie Langtry, who had studied the Suzuki method in Japan. Sister Marie took her violin to all the classrooms of the primary school touting for students, just as Mrs Turner had done at the swings in Shropshire. Anne went home and begged her mum to start learning the violin; as Anne says, she loved it right from the start and wanted to play all the time, even though her brothers would beg her to stop. Anne eventually became a professional player and teacher, working for Education Queensland in Brisbane. But something wasn't right.

'It got to the point where teaching felt like a slog. It's hard to teach the joy of music if you just feel exhausted, and I wanted to be inspired in a deeper way.'

Bear in mind the working day of an instrumental strings teacher.

They will start with early morning String Orchestra rehearsal, where they need to tune around thirty instruments. Then they can have possibly nine students (in a mix of cello, viola, bass or violin) for half-hour lessons throughout the day. Half-hours in which they need to check and tune thirty-six different strings, check nine bows for rosin and condition, organise stands and chairs and possible tears and sulks, and then try to learn something in the short time they have left. Add to that administrative work, buying and maintaining instruments, arranging, buying and printing music, organising concerts and extra rehearsals and you can understand why it is a challenging environment for teachers. Anne knew that if she carried on in the same way she would be burnt out in a matter of years, so she stopped teaching music and began to study for a masters in counselling.

'I started to miss teaching. I realised it was more in me to teach than to be a counsellor, so I tried to look for different ways of teaching, not completely changing my career. It had never occurred to me to start Bardon Strings, but I went back to Suzuki teaching and had a lot of adult students. I was loving teaching the adults, then a friend of mine who'd taken up cello as an adult said she had given up because there was no ensemble to play in for her level, so why didn't I start one? Then I thought, this is a fantastic avenue: I can use the ideas I have about wanting to nurture not just the musical side. People have all these insecurities and things we accumulate over our lives from our childhood. Maybe they've given out to people all their lives and thought it was about time they nurtured something within themselves, and through this they choose music only later in life.'

Anne's big, grey-blue eyes soften at the memory.

'I have experienced insecurity and anxiety at times and I wanted this to be a place where people feel safe, because I know what it's like to feel unsafe. It's so easy to feel unsafe playing music; you can be so exposed. I wanted everyone to know it's okay to make mistakes, we're here to enjoy being with each other and making music.'

This is an extract from an email Anne sent to the new players, giving information about the first rehearsal:

We have seven musicians coming along to connect and play music. Playing with others can be one of the most satisfying and enjoyable aspects of playing a musical instrument. Trying anything new can be both exciting and daunting at the same time so congratulate yourself for stepping out of your comfort zone' towards a new experience which has the potential to nourish and extend you in many ways.

On 2 June 2016, seven players, students of friends, turned up at Anne's townhouse: one double bassist, four cellists and two violinists. Anne moved most of her furniture out of her lounge onto the verandah to make space, and then they arranged themselves in a semi-circle and began. What did they play?

'I was very conscious of not putting anything in front of them that made them think I was treating them like a child. I tried to find things that would make them feel respected. We played a scale to warm up, then an African round that I had really enjoyed, so I thought they would too. At the end, they said, "We had so much fun!"'

Ensemble playing was new for Anne's students, but it was also a whole new adventure for Anne; she had to find her way as well. Anne likens the experience to parenting. But just as she had worked out what her students needed within the orchestra for their best development, they would move ahead and she would have to recalibrate for their new abilities and confidence.

One of the challenges of teaching beginner players of any age is the areas you choose to correct and develop. Is it sound, intonation, rhythm, phrasing or playing together? Dropping a big weight suddenly onto a glass table will smash it, but if you add the same weight slowly the glass top will support it, so Anne had to consider every week what to work on, how much weight to add and what to leave for later.

'When they first started, I used to let a multitude of stuff go by. If we could just get it moderately together ... Then I had this recognition that they had got onto a higher level, so I can be more critical now. I can't keep treating them like babies, because they won't get enough out of it. I have to respect them.'

Over the years, Anne has noticed a huge change in the players' confidence. She talks about Luke, the leader of the orchestra, who plays solos and adds his own embellishments, and whose sound has improved enormously over the years. Ray, whose rhythm now sparkles. Bronwyn, who has been there from the first rehearsal and plays like a powerful engine as the single bass player.

Anne has let me come along and play with Bardon Strings, so I sit in the viola section with Cae, Kylie, Claire and Lisa, and we prepare for *Ring of Fire*, a triumphant fantasy piece by Kathryn Griesinger. Anne lifts her baton and gathers the attention of the consultant doctors, research scientists, school principals and lawyers, the attention of people who are wildly successful in their professional careers and yet are willing to play this high school–level music, and off we go. The cellos and bass begin, an ominous repeated note on their low strings, then the violas join with the same rhythm, and finally the violins enter with an intense, dark melody. I have played in quite a few professional orchestras and was not expecting these amateur musicians to sound the same. But they do. The integrity of their intention means their music flows from them in powerful, undeniable waves. As we play, I glance around at the different players and notice everyone has the same look on their face – complete concentration. No other time matters except the time of *Ring of Fire*. They are immersed in music. As the musicians play, the footballers and gymnasts walk past the open windows and stare in, drawn to the furnace. Little girls dance and older people watch wistfully, wondering if this too could be their story.

I am hooked. I ask Anne if I can keep playing with Bardon Strings each week, and she says yes.

From toddlers to teenagers, five years on from that fateful evening in June there are now more than forty members of Bardon Strings, and Anne has just started a new group for beginners. Among them are a diplomat, a chemist, a senior civil servant and a civil engineer, all giving something to themselves after all these years.

Anne says it perfectly: 'I didn't even know it was going to work, but here we are, five years later. They must be working hard at home, because I can hear the change in their playing.

And everyone comes away saying how much they've enjoyed it. That has to mean I'm on the right track.'

Georgie is not yet a civil engineer or a diplomat, nor indeed a chemist. Georgie is six years old and wants to be an astronaut. Georgie loves to sing, as high and as loud as she can. She throws her head back and her mouth, a cartoon of tonsils and uvula and no front teeth, releases a sweep of music. Georgie sings a song, then picks up her violin and plays the song again, note for note.

This is not a miracle; it is not a talent. Sure, you might say Georgie is lucky because she has been brought up with music – her dad plays the guitar, her mum plays the cello and her sister plays the clarinet – but Georgie works hard. She plays hard. She listens to music every day and already she can perceive the finest differences between pitches and emotions. With that level of attention already developed, it is no surprise that Georgie displays a very high emotional intelligence. So much so that she understands the complexities of different cultures and once uttered to me the great wisdom that if Australians think other cultures are odd, surely other cultures must think we are odd, and doesn't that just make us all the same?

Learning music isn't always easy, though. Georgie curls her toes when I give her a new piece and wails and says it's too hard, but she dives into the tricky bits first, and once they are learnt, it all feels easy. And once that feels easy, the piece she had wailed at before that one feels even easier, and so Georgie is even more confident about playing it.

I ask Georgie if she would like to play at the end-of-year concert at school. She played at the last class concert in front of about thirty people and thinks I mean the same thing.

'Sure!' She grins, tucking her violin into bed with its blankie.

I only realise my error when I see the look on her face as she turns up to the concert, and there are five hundred parents and students in the school hall.

'Mr Ed, I thought you meant the concert like last year?'

I feel dreadful. As a teacher, this is a calamity. Even though Georgie is playing beautifully, I cannot help but think of my own experience when I was the same age as her. At a school Christmas concert with Mrs Turner I played the solo in *Good King Wenceslas*, became overwhelmed by the audience, completely stuffed it up and never really recovered. What if the same happens with Georgie?

Georgie's mum, Cathy, saves me. She grabs her dear child and squeezes the nerves out of her, tiny rib by tiny rib. She whispers some magic elixir into her ear and Georgie and I walk out on stage to perform *Go Tell Aunt Rhody*.

Georgie's performance stills the hot, fractious mob of parents and children. Her sound rings out from her tiny violin and it is impossible to not be grabbed by her musical intention. Georgie, in just a few notes, smashes it.

With her music, with every new note, with every step onto

the stage, Georgie discovers her own bravery. Music builds a fortress of courage in her heart.

———————

How can it get any better than this?

This is a phrase Charlie often says, especially when things are going well. At first I was confused and wondered if it wasn't a little greedy to ask for more from life when already we are so fortunate, but her response was surprising.

'We ask how it can get any better than this, and the universe shows us how. If we ask how it can get any worse, we will also be shown.'

I am sceptical but start to try it with my playing and teaching. And it works.

———————

Ben is a new adult student, which is wonderful for me, because I can bend him to my will. That sounds a little weird but teaching someone from the start is much easier in terms of teaching technique and philosophical approach.

I chat with Ben via email and arrange a date for his first cello lesson. He brings a cello (useful), *Suzuki Cello School, Volume 1*, Joanne Martin's *I Can Read Music* and a notebook.

One of the great challenges of learning as an adult is the bravery to put yourself in a position of ignorance after spending a few decades becoming an expert in your chosen career. Among my adult students I have an anaesthetist, an ethics adviser, a school principal, a pathologist and an Eastern religions philosopher. All these adults are willing to come to their lessons and play the same pieces as the seven- or ten-year-olds before them. I am constantly in awe of their lack of ego. Their bravery to move from a place of competence to incompetence.

Ben is from Germany and played accordion as a child but always wanted to learn the cello. I begin Ben's first lesson in the same way as Rosie's, asking why he chose the cello.

The sound. It is always the sound. And a fear of regretting not starting it, even in his early fifties. Ben is a scientist and presumably has his own bank account, so now he can do what he wants. After going through the names of the cello bits and practising sitting, Ben makes his first sounds on the instrument.

I play and he copies: a simple rhythm on the D string, ti-ti-ta, just plucking with our right hand. The sound he makes is round and careful.

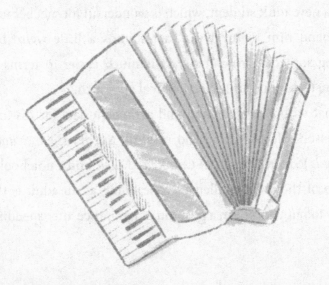

'Ben, ask yourself: how can you make your sound … happier?' (I never use the words better or worse.) 'How can it be more comfortable? Listen again …'

And I play again, making sure my plucked D is as gorgeous and vibrant as it can be.

Ben copies again and it is a whole new world. Already. Open, and this time generous and full of joy.

He plays again, thwacks the string in the wrong direction and it twangs against the fingerboard. Ben recoils with laughter and I remind him that this is an adventure, and unlike learning to be a pilot, no-one dies if you stuff up. As I wonder what a pilot instructor says in moments like these, we try again.

After plucking the cello strings, I go through some bow-hold exercises with Ben and we prepare ourselves for the first bow strokes on the cello. It's tempting to think the left hand, which makes the different notes on the cello, is the hard part of playing. Really, it's the bow – that's where the sound, the expression, the music comes from, so it needs specific attention right from the start.

Once again, I play a small rhythm to Ben and he copies: tikka-tikka-ti-ti.

So much of learning to play an instrument is understanding our own complexity and desires. It demands a huge amount of courage to confront ourselves with something physically and mentally and spiritually new, especially something as demanding as playing an instrument. One of the holes (not the f-hole on the front of the cello) we can fall into as adult beginners is to judge ourselves harshly, so harshly that we never actually get started. Music, at any level, needs to flow to work. It needs to breathe to live.

I play and Ben plays, but he stops after one go, making a comment about not sounding like Yo-Yo Ma on his Stradivarius. On the one hand, it is a great advantage to know the sound you are aiming for, but on the other hand, it can be a disadvantage if you compare yourself savagely with that sound. A beautiful, complex, full and mature sound comes from making a big block of sound and refining it. Michelangelo did not create his sculpture of *David* by sticking a bunch of little stones together. He carved it from an enormous block, and that's what we need to do as musicians. We need a very, very big sound block.

Our musical pilgrimage is to listen to ourselves as acutely as possible, and it is our privilege, as musicians, to follow that path. We can begin this in our very first lesson, but simply buying a better instrument, like Yo-Yo Ma's Stradivarius, is not going to help. Musicians are used to making an excellent sound on an average instrument. We spend many years playing on student instruments that are well made but do not mean your parents need to mortgage the house and cash in their pension. When we grow up and decide to spend thousands of dollars on a new viola/horn/recorder, we are ready. We have developed the technique to draw richness from our instrument, and along with that we have developed a desire and technique for good intonation, smoothness and sweetness. It all takes time, so much time, but I cannot imagine time being better spent.

I repeat to Ben what Peter Luff says about playing: 'You need to get the car started to tune the engine.'

Ben puts his bow on the D string and the car starts. It's a Mercedes-Benz in the making.

———————————

One piece to listen to and fully absorb the importance of quality of sound is Arvo Pärt's *Spiegel im Spiegel*, or *Mirror in the Mirror*. An Estonian composer now in his mid-eighties, back in the 1970s Pärt had a personal crisis that led to him not knowing what music *meant* anymore. Imagine words becoming incomprehensible, or losing the sense of taste, or an expression on your partner's face being unreadable. It must have felt like he was losing his mind. And this was not a short crisis that was over in a weekend. It lasted nearly a decade. As Pärt said, he did not know anymore what was a key (the landscape you compose a piece in if you're Beethoven or Mozart), or what the intervals, or spaces, were between notes. Pärt says of this time that he felt he was losing his inner compass. He had been a successful composer but he was musically silent during these lost years. As he came to a new style he said it was a step into poverty, but the new style, which he named tintinnabuli, became one of the most listened to and most copied styles of the late twentieth and early twenty-first centuries. Tintinnabuli is a minimalist style of music, where changes happen subtly and slowly, the notes are few and far between, and the feeling is one of an ever-expanding horizon. The name comes from the Latin for bell and seems to garner profound spirituality and humanity in a simple chord.

As you listen to *Spiegel*, or rather, as you succumb to *Spiegel*, the simple line of the music exerts an increasing pressure on your heart. It becomes undeniable, like the weight of a child who has come to you to be hugged. Think of Pablo Picasso and his line drawings, single lines that encompass the entire arc of life, or the scathing, minimal words of the poet Philip Larkin, who denigrates and celebrates a scene with a single line. Those artists' works are mirrored in the music of Arvo Pärt.

———————————

The sound we make as musicians, and the sound we experience as listeners, is the single most important thing for me. As a player, you can play as fast or as loud or as emotionally as you want, but if the quality of the sound isn't there, no-one will want to listen. So it is even more devastating if we are very nervous when we go out on stage, because the first thing to deteriorate is our sound.

Zoe Knighton is a professional cellist and one of the founding members of the Flinders Quartet, one of Australia's leading string quartets. She gives regular solo recitals and is known especially for her sound, but it hasn't been an easy path.

'In my early professional life, I suffered complete paralysis of stage fright. One of the things that got me out of it was trusting my own sound. One of the things I do every day, which I've done for years now, is to find my sound of the day. To be honest, it's slightly different every day because I'm slightly different and my cello's slightly different, and it's about finding a sound that I feel some kind of affinity with. And that requires a level of listening that for me is almost like meditating.'

Zoe's quick, intelligent face turns inwards.

'When I'm focusing on my own sound in an effective way, I feel a glorious stillness and oneness in my mind. Just feeling comfortable with who I am as a person. That way I don't worry so much about what I have to play technically on the cello, it just becomes about the sound and listening. Now my way out of nerves is simply to listen.

'I remember one of my teachers saying to me, don't try to be someone else, just be yourself in the sound.'

————————————————

Through listening to myself and others play over these decades, music has taught me the truth of sound. We cannot develop if the sound does not move freely, if the music does not ring true. The sound will always show you what needs to change – finger position, bow speed or your own attitude. And once you listen to yourself and your sensitivity deepens, you may notice a feeling of not ringing true in your life, not moving freely through your existence. Through listening we find what we need, not what we want. We find something needs to change. Through listening we find the bravery to make that change.

This was the process I went through with accepting my own transgender identity.

One of the great gifts of being transgender is the space to rebuild our lives exactly how we dream. Or at least we can try.

We rename ourselves. We claim the bodies we knew were ours all along. We place ourselves in the world according to *our* beliefs, not those of our parents, our siblings, our teachers or our contemporaries. We change our sound and ask to be listened to in a new way. If you are not transgender, or are not close to anyone who is, it is hard to describe just how terrifying this can be. Just as the horn is walking a tightrope on stilettos, so is transitioning to the gender you know you are. If you knew how hard it was going to be at the start you might never take that first step, and it is a path so few have taken before us. To be transgender in this age is to be a pioneer; doctors still have no idea why we exist, but the fact is we do. We are undeniable and we have our own voices, voices that sound as we want them to. We ask to not only be heard but to be listened to.

I went to a state selective girls school. I grew up being told to be careful at night and to never be alone with a man. I grew up with the fears and delights of the female world, but as I listened to myself, I realised I was transgender.

Just as the skills I forged as a musician matured with introspection, time and profound thought, so did the realisation of my gender identity; both came into focus with the same process. I began my gender transition just before my fiftieth birthday. A little later than many, but better late than never.

It took a long time to say, but now I can. I am a transgender man.

I found my bravery through music.

B:
KNOWLEDGE

We are born knowing
everything and slowly
forget it.

CHINESE PROVERB

(as relayed by Mrs Izod,
my Year 7 maths teacher)

WHY DO WE HAVE A DESIRE to gain knowledge? Why do we read books, listen to lectures, watch how-to videos, go to music lessons? Why do we ask questions? Is it merely to earn more money, appear more intelligent and escape deeper psychological challenges, or is there something higher involved? Might Mrs Izod and her Year 7 Chinese proverb be correct, that by seeking knowledge we are seeking a more profound knowledge of ourselves? Even a knowledge of something beyond ourselves?

Throughout my childhood, gaining knowledge seemed to be inspired by one of two things: curiosity and obligation. Thanks to excellent state school teachers, my curiosity was often piqued before I realised there was also an obligation to learn something. I was curious how to write well, and Mrs Castle, with her dreadful teeth and smoker's voice, satisfied that curiosity with the obligatory knowledge of how to parse a sentence. I was curious where I and my place, Shropshire, sat in the world, and Mrs Williams satisfied that curiosity with geography and Mrs Johns with history and Miss Spicer with literature. Things I was less curious about – building plastic boxes and netball – remained foggy and indistinct to me. Curiosity didn't kill my cat, it just made it stronger.

Like an art teacher who puts out a block of clay as a provocation for a class of six-year-olds, I play my viola or cello in a music lesson and watch as the student is provoked into questions. What is that wiggly thing you are doing with your hand? How can you move your bow so fast? How do you play two notes at the same time? Why does that note sound louder than that one? Why are you bald?

When a music student asks questions, when they show curiosity, I know we are going to progress together in a certain way. Not to say a better way, or an easier way, but perhaps a more accessible way. When a student asks questions, they are showing a healthy mind. When a student asks nothing and merely accepts and repeats, I worry there are other stresses in their lives. What is the opposite of curiosity? Morbidity? Apathy? Indifference? Words that show a mind in dis-ease.

Going through a bleak period of depression (is there any other kind?) in 2014 was the only time I had no curiosity. I had comprehensively lost my care for anything, particularly myself, so why bother asking questions, or reading books, or improving something, anything, nothing? Depression is the bully and leader of a gang of hideous characters – callousness, weariness, disregard – and they all came and crowded in on me and simply would not rest until I had surrendered to them all, one by dreadful one. But there was a single thing that got me out of that mess, one single thing that saved from me from killing myself: the hope of teaching music again.

Curiosity is a playmate in life. It takes us on unpredictable adventures and leads us on to heavenly escarpments. How can we live our lives without being curious?

'When you stop being curious, that's when you stop being a good teacher.'

Edwina is a teacher for children with additional needs; she is also one of my cello students and has just made the best summary of curiosity's gifts.

And Edwina's own curiosity has grown stronger with music.

Edwina started playing the cello a couple of years ago. She had some singing lessons as a child, but learning cello was a whole new destination for her. Edwina says how, with her cello, she can literally feel bits of her brain turning on as she plays. Edwina is a dedicated student and practises for about forty minutes every day; she starts with bow hold exercises then bell notes, getting the cello to resonate as fully as possible, goes on to revision and polishing her older pieces, and then and only then practises her new piece. It's demanding, day in and day out, but it also brings Edwina much joy and some unexpected benefits. As Edwina spends time learning and practising and repeating fundamentals, it mirrors the learning of her own students with additional needs and reminds her just how important those fundamentals are.

As Edwina says, 'My philosophy has been to remain curious, and to remain interested in what is going on around me. Because I've seen throughout my profession that those teachers who have lost that curiosity, they can become very bitter and disgruntled and lose the very quality that made them a good teacher in the first place. It's very easy to go down that road, even after decades of teaching.'

It strikes us both how being curious allows a closer emotional connection with a young student, as that quality is so natural in children.

'Cello reminds me what it's like to learn something for the very first time, because I don't come from a musical background, I don't come from a musical family. So I look at my students and think how far they've come, as they don't have that background, that exposure to reading or writing, and yet they come to school and they are expected to reach a certain benchmark. They are on the back foot before they've even started.

Edwina hugs her cello, the instrument a comfort as she speaks.

'I associate learning music with learning to read, so I can have a greater appreciation of how it is for those kids to process words. You need those foundations, you need those fundamentals; a lot of the kids I teach, they are missing those learning blocks. I think cello has improved me, given me more understanding and empathy as a teacher.'

To begin playing an instrument takes curiosity, and to continue to play, to improve, to go deeper takes curiosity through a lifetime of practice.

Music can teach you curiosity, but it's not a given. And when a musician loses their curiosity, it's a wretched scene.

In my twenties, I played viola in the Hong Kong Philharmonic Orchestra. The orchestra was going through a time of change with new players, but there were still a few of the less enthusiastic players left, one American bassoonist in particular. Now, the bassoon is not an instrument that comes to mind when you think of shining moments in music, apart from the opening of Stravinsky's *The Rite of Spring*, which is pretty much the best piece of music ever written. There, the bassoon sings high at the top of its range, a ponderous bird flying close to the sun. But much of the time the bassoon is like the viola – a binder, a supporter and an enrichment for the main tune. So when the bassoon does have the tune it's a big moment, and bassoonists, like all other instrumentalists, have these major parts of their repertoire well practised and ready to go. Not this bassoonist.

Rodrigo's *Concierto de Aranjuez* for guitar and orchestra is one of those pieces that when I find out someone hasn't heard it, I feel a little envious, knowing they still have the first time ahead of them. It is sumptuous, it is jaunty, it is full of thrill and happiness. In short, it is sunshine in sound. The music is acrobats perfectly moving over and under each other, but one mistimed jump and all is lost. Most important in the music is the jaunt, making sure the pulse stays strong and playful. Right from the beginning the guitar scuppers your sense of where the pulse is – are there two big beats in a bar, or three? When pulse changes like that it gives a syncopated feel, and it's even more important that the overall pulse stays very, very steady. You can try it now: tap your foot to the speed of a second, then say ti-ti for each tap. Now say eas-i-ly to each tap. Fun, right? Now you're a musician.

The night of the concert. We arrived at the bassoon spot, not anticipating the car crash about to happen. As the first movement comes to an end there is an explosion of chords from the guitar, then the bassoon and the trumpet hand the music from one to another, shadowing the guitar's notes and ideally bringing the music to an elegant landing. The bassoonist without curiosity, the bassoonist who had stopped practising a long time ago (and who doesn't play at all anymore) did the equivalent of sitting down in the middle of the acrobatic act and putting a leg out to trip everyone else up. He began to play but entered with such shoddy rhythm and pulse that all that flawless momentum that had been built up vanished; he had brought the music's sinus rhythm to atrial fibrillation. It was a shameful moment. You could hear the orchestra gasp as one player wrecked the whole ship. The audience seemed bludgeoned by the mediocrity. Was that how it was meant to end? Fortunately, the conductor managed to haul everyone together for the last few notes, and instead of an elegant landing, we came to a shuddering halt. The bassoonist, uncuriously, left the orchestra at the end of the year.

We display different types of curiosity but satisfying them gives the same reward – a little shot of dopamine. There is diversive curiosity, which gives you the desire to experience something new, epistemic curiosity, where you feel a hole in your knowledge about a composer, a cuisine, an intellectual pursuit, and you deepen your knowledge in that field, and empathic curiosity, when you feel a need to understand another person's life and character. The beauty of music, especially learning an instrument, is that all three types of curiosity are utilised, and so the reward, dopamine, is a triple shot.

Since my first horn lesson with Peter Luff, I have been practising and practising, for an hour every day. My neighbours could not be more grateful and say polite things like, 'Ed, your tone is getting more … solid.' Or, 'What time do you practise, usually?', car keys and suitcase in hand.

All I can think is what I'll buy them for Christmas, to say thank you for not stealing my horn and giving it to the Salvation Army for their instrument appeal. Happy, our four-kilo bitzer dog, is distinctly unhappy. She has taken to retreating to the back of her kennel and building an acoustic wall with her doggie toys. Charlie, meanwhile, retains her

Buddhist calm and puts on her noise-cancelling headphones. 'Eadric, you'll be playing with the Queensland Symphony in no time at all.'

I return to Peter for another lesson, feeling pretty pleased with myself. At the end of my first lesson Peter had sent me away with a book of beginner studies by a man called, I kid you not, Anton Horner. Seriously. This isn't nominative determinism, this is just nominative. Anton was an Austrian violinist who only took up the horn as a second instrument at music college. It clearly went well as he ended up first horn with the Philadelphia Orchestra and played with them for nearly fifty years. I have studied the first two pages of his studies and I'm rocking it.

Or am I?

One of the great challenges of learning an instrument at any age is to do things as well as possible, right from the start, and not to cut corners. Unfortunately, bad habits come first because they are easier, and I already have some bad habits.

In my practice over the last couple of weeks, I have started the same way every day: suck the finger, spit the seed, buzz on the mouthpiece, deflate into the horn. I then play from the beginning of the study book, with a middle C, going up through the harmonic series to an E and the next overtone, a G, all done with the embouchure and diaphragm. With the use of the valves I have added a D, F and A. But being a Type-A personality with a robust ego, I may have also flicked through to later pages in the book and had a little go at things like the solo from Brahms' first symphony, or seen how high I can go if I blow super hard and clamp the horn to my lips as much as possible. It's the equivalent of a learner driver stealing a Formula One car, because they want to 'see what it feels like'. There's curiosity, and there's foolhardiness.

I play a note that I consider a high C, and as I play, Peter subtly pulls the horn away from my mouth. I try to follow it and the note ends up spluttering to a halt like an engine with no petrol.

'Ed, don't use so much pressure. You're cutting off the blood supply to your lips.'

Ah, that's why they are going blue. I try again and realise the pressure was keeping my lips tight and now I cannot get anywhere near my 'high' C, which I have just found out is a very middling C.

'Remember, the horn is an instrument you cannot rush. If you want to learn quickly, you've chosen the wrong instrument.'

At which point I want to fall into a horn-shaped hole in the ground and never, ever come out, not even if the horn is calling me. I realise that over the last week my ego has been pushing me to go faster and louder and higher than I am ready for, and all I have done is develop bad habits, habits I now need to undo. Thank heavens I have an excellent teacher to help. I resolve to go back to the beginning. Since I've only been playing for a week, I won't have to go very far.

Suck the finger, spit the seed, breathe using my diaphragm, deflate from the bottom of my breath.

Peter sends me away with a twinkly yet serious reminder to not try to progress too fast.

'Remember the process. Follow the process and you are bound to be successful.'

_____

'Do the practice and all is coming.'

As I develop my ritual of music practice each morning, I rediscover my love for discipline and order.

I get up early, have a coffee and a walk with Happy and Charlie, meditate for an hour, then I'm ready for practice. My neighbours are ready as well; they have left the area. I blow into the mouthpiece first and make sure I still have a pair of lips, then off I go into the world of harmonics. Not to dwell on it too much but one of the reasons the horn has such a fearsome reputation for difficulty is that we are playing at the top end of the harmonic series. You remember the first few overtones after the fundamental – the octave, the fifth, then another octave? After that the intervals, or spaces between the notes, go to a third, another octave, a smaller third called a minor third, another octave, then those intervals keep getting smaller. You can imagine it like a path. Most of the other brass instruments play at the nice wide part of the path, where you can run around and not fall into the crocodile-filled river alongside. Horn players do not play here. They play at the narrow end of the path where the barrier has collapsed, the path is crumbling and the crocodiles are hungry and snapping.

So, as I learn the horn I observe the rituals that horn players follow every day. We need to warm up and exercise the embouchure and diaphragm by playing up through the harmonic series, as high as we can. Peter calls the exercises 'elevators'. As you can see, it's a perfect exercise for a Type-A personality, but to do it properly we need to do it without ego, without pressing. Without trying too hard. I'm learning a lot about myself; namely, I am impatient and egotistical yet pragmatic. I try to practise without judgement, merely observation, and listen to the Chicago Symphony Orchestra playing Wagner's *Siegfried's Funeral March* for inspiration. It's amazing how a good funeral march can enliven you. I have also noticed I spend a considerable amount of time trying to remove condensation from my horn. It becomes such a habit after a few weeks that I start to do the same with my viola and wonder why there's no water dribbling from the f-holes. Well, apart from that one time.

I return to Peter after a couple of weeks and he is pleased. Some teachers heap praise on you and it becomes meaningless, and others give it so rarely it becomes deflating, but Peter gives the perfect amount. I get a 'good' or two for my home note C, and as we scale the harmonic ladder I even get an 'excellent' for my high C. Okay, a middling C. Very middling.

As a special treat, Peter plays a duet with me. It's the music equivalent of stepping into a Bentley and being whisked off to a luxury hotel when you're used to cycling everywhere and staying in a tent. It is simply glorious. I tag along with Peter's heroic sound and feel like I am born again, then Peter pops his horn back onto his mouth and plays two simple notes: the very bottom and the very top of the horn's enormous range, four and a half octaves apart. Peter distils hundreds of thousands of hours of practice into that tiny moment. To put it into perspective, after a month I can barely play one octave, and your average singer might have a range of two octaves. If you want to play four and a half octaves on the trumpet, you buy a higher instrument. The horn is a phenomenon, an enigma, a koan in sound.

Repetition, process, repetition, order, repetition, discipline, repetition. As the weeks go by, the horn seems to soften, to meld more easily into my lips, and the notes spring rather than stutter to life and sound less like a rhinoceros calling a friend for raucous sexy times.

The Brisbane Chamber Choir gives a concert at St John's Cathedral in Brisbane. Graeme Morton, its founder and director, has asked me to host the concert, which means I get to chat to the audience from the pulpit. The concert is exquisite and includes *The Lamb* by John Tavener, a setting to music of the poem by William Blake.

Little Lamb who made thee
Dost thou know who made thee
Gave thee life and bid thee feed.

As the sopranos offer the opening phrase and the basses fall under them in ecstasy, I look around the cathedral, started in the early 1900s and finished only ten years ago. At the east end the stone is cut by hand, and at the west end it is cut by computer-guided laser. In the pulpit, the flocks of vicars and speakers who have climbed in and out over the decades have left a shine on the stones around the opening. This mark initially seems like a stain, a diminishing, but is actually a polishing of the stone from the repeated touching of it. I remember seeing this before in a sheep-shearing shed in southeast Queensland, a place called Nundubbermere. The shed, like the cathedral, is over a hundred years old and the wooden pens for the sheep all have a line of the same mark around them, exactly at sheep height. A sheen of lanolin from the sheep who, just like the vicars and speakers, have polished the wood to a high gleam over the decades. The truth of the wood, its grain, is revealed both in pattern and texture.

I reach out and touch the stone in the pulpit and feel the extreme smoothness, thanks to the repetition of actions over and over again across generations, the same process, the same discipline, and wonder at the beauty that has come through this reiteration.

And it is the same with music, listening to it again and again, listening to the same music at the same points in our lives, music of tradition, Christmas carols and evening lullabies and anniversary songs, and how these sounds become a scaffolding of our memories, the repetition of traditions a new ring of life on our family tree, and how music, with its repetition through practice and performance, rubs onto us and brings a sheen and a lustre and a truth to our lives.

———————————————

What is knowledge? If you look at the etymology of the word, one of its original meanings is to have wisdom of something through bringing it into the world. In other words, to know something properly, you need to do it.

'I want to learn the viola. I'm seventy-two. Is that too old?'

'I want my son to learn the cello. He's five. Is that too young?'

I am a cello and viola teacher and recently received these two requests.

What is the answer?

I shall never say seventy-two is too old for anything. Neither is eighty-two, or a hundred and two. And many children are already playing complex pieces at the age of five. The only things that change are how we learn, and from that, what we learn. And at some point, we might find the answer to that almost unanswerable question: why we learn.

There are as many ways of learning music as there are

students in a class. You can learn to read rhythm notation first, then pitch notation, and take those notes to your instrument. You can learn music through matching different notes to different colours. You can learn to sing first, or you can learn from a YouTube video or teach yourself from a library book. You can learn the outline of your instrument and fill in the gaps, or you can learn each note, one by one. You can learn with your head, your heart, or your spirit. Or you can do a combination of all these. Every student learns in their own way, but if we recognise music as a language, one of the most direct ways to learn music is simply through listening and copying. This is commonly how we have learnt to speak our own languages, through immersion and repetition. If we do this from birth, we hardly remember any challenge. If we do this as an adult, we may become impatient with the time taken and want to move things along a bit. Or a lot. Adults who learn the easiest put aside their adult preconceptions and egos and play as a child. They learn as a child.

To listen, to truly listen, takes a huge amount of energy and honesty. To listen beyond just hearing sounds, to listen actively to the world we must open, we must surrender, we must soften and relinquish assumption. To listen we need to be quiet within and still our own voice, and that is rare and enigmatic.

But we can always try. Practice, right? How about now … Put a timer on for a minute, close your eyes, and concentrate solely on the information given to you by your ears. What can you hear? Can you hear anything beyond your own thoughts and feelings of discomfort? Perhaps a minute isn't long enough. Try five minutes and now feel what happens. As your thoughts give way, or as your self gives way, do you notice more sounds, more detail, a greater perception of dimension? And if you keep going in the same direction, it just gets better and better. Sometimes that's all we need, isn't it? Just to keep going in the same direction.

In music lessons, I keep my students from reading music for quite a few weeks, or, if they are very young, a few months. If a student starts to equate music with black marks on a page, and to play music they must read those black dots with their logical brain and translate that into a physical action, then music, the true inner music, can easily be lost. You have had to go outside yourself to come in again. Whereas if you teach a student through listening and copying alone and they do not look at the written music until they have learnt a piece, they play much more freely and understand music as a language, not as a series of dots and lines. Imagine learning a language through only reading it from a book and never hearing it and you'll immediately understand the difference. A lesson always goes better when music is kept in its original form as sound alone. Of course, reading music needs to come in at some point, but not until a student feels the music from the inside. Otherwise a student will always be limited by what they can read, not what they can imagine.

Rosie, my seven-year-old cello student, is sitting eagerly with her cello, so comfortable with it she looks like she's waiting for the conductor to come on stage with the Berlin Philharmonic.

Rosie is a delight to teach. She greets me with glee each week and does a little dance around her chair before we bow to each other and sit. Rosie has developed a challenging wiggly jumping bow, which I'm a little concerned may put my back out at some point, but I give it my best middle-aged shot. After a variety of bows, we start the lesson.

We begin slowly and play our bell notes, listening carefully to hear who has the longer vibration. There's a truly beautiful phenomenon in music, in everything, that links one vibration to another. The phenomenon is called sympathetic vibration and occurs when one note is played and stimulates a vibration through the air of another surface. It's most strongly seen when the notes match, or when they are close on the harmonic series – octaves, fourths or fifths. I show my students a magic trick where I play a C on my G string and, if it is perfectly in tune, the C string starts to vibrate as well. This is happening all the time when people play – the better the placing of the notes, the intonation, the better the sound, the tone. So intonation means 'in sound'. It seems like an advanced concept that you may save for a much later stage, but it is so important to sow those seeds of listening and to know what to listen for at this early stage. You can even feel the vibrations through your left hand as well. Rosie, in her first month of playing, can do it brilliantly; we can all do it at any stage, we only need to be made aware.

I'm aware of sympathetic vibration when I meet new people and feel the vibrations from them – are our vibrations flowing together, or is there a bump? And when I'm feeling out of kilter, I find my own vibrations fight against themselves and others, even to the point of not being able to play so well in tune.

After Rosie's and my ears and hands are woken up, we play Simon Says. Or, since I'm a strong feminist from my years of living as a girl, Simona Says.

Simona says … I play short phrases, building the complexity from rhythms on one open string to two strings, then adding some notes with the fingers of the left hand. Rosie is improving at the game every week and we now add subtleties of dynamics, forte and piano, then mega loud, as Rosie shouts out 'fortississississississimo' as loudly as her child bellows allow.

We head into our new piece for the week. Rosie learns her pieces by ear, then we look at how the music is written. Today it's *Campfire Glow*, a masterpiece of pedagogy in the *Encore on Strings* book. The best pedagogy allows every student to gain each skill with tiny, imperceptible steps, so when you look back, a journey of ten thousand miles has been taken, but hardly noticed. Even on such a boundless journey, the student greets you with glee.

———————————

When I was a kid, I used to listen to the Grieg Piano Concerto with Gran'ma. Mum was in the kitchen roasting Sunday lunch, and my siblings were out and about with their own stories. But my story on a Sunday was always Gran'ma. I would ask her to tell me tales of life in the far-flung universe of the Second World War; Gran'ma seemed so ancient to my eight-year-old self (she would have been sixty-six), so these tales of battle and verve were addictive stuff.

Stories of sitting in a third-class railway carriage, on Gran'ma's lap a whole suitcase of precious eggs, all individually wrapped – loot from a trip to visit Mum in Devon where she had been evacuated. Stories of being a fire warden in London, sitting on the rooftops of buildings in the East End, waiting throughout the night for the Nazi bombers to come and then call out the fires to the fire brigade below. Stories of running with a water-filled rubbish bin to put out an incendiary attack on the Midland Bank. Stories of rationing and cabbage and cycling to the coast for escape. Stories of poverty and simplicity, of deep love, fun, acceptance and stoic fight.

And after all the adventures, as the slow movement of the Grieg arrived, a calm would settle over Gran'ma. She would sit in her favourite chair, the eggs in a suitcase replaced by a pre-lunch sweet sherry resting on her box-pleat tweed skirt, and she would speak about her garden, about Grandpa's rhubarb and roses, and how the birds would sing each morning no matter how many bombs had dropped, nor how many people had died the night before during the Blitz.

Gran'ma would evoke the damp and fog of London winters, summer hedgerows taller than churches, and the mists coming over the Devon moors in autumn. She would describe the sunshine of a trip to the sea and coming back with her face covered in blisters. (Gran'ma was auburn, and burn she did.)

It was a time, as she said, when small things mattered. When small things became everything. When sometimes only nature had something positive to give.

We sat and we listened to the Grieg as Gran'ma repeated her war stories and I would ask to hear them again and again, each time adding my own remembering of the telling of the stories until they became a palimpsest of both her memories and mine. I heard the stories and the music countless times, and each time I listened I fell into a deeper connection with Gran'ma, until the story barely needed to be told for there to be one anyway. The listening and repetition had rubbed off on me and left a mark, a shine, so much so that Gran'ma's essence vibrates inside me still as I think about where we might be going, and what we will need to carry on our laps.

_____

'There's your high register, your low register and your mid register – your cash register. These studies are your cash register.'

Peter is referring to the glories of the horn repertoire and those solos that sear themselves into your heart, and to the Horner (I still can't get over that name) studies I am now about halfway through. I have been listening obsessively to Tchaikovsky's fifth symphony and the horn solo in the slow movement. Tchaikovsky had huge misgivings about this symphony and wrote frequently to his friends and his patron, Nadezhda von Meck, with his worries the symphony would be no good: he was empty, too old (he was barely fifty) and written out. Isn't it amazing how we can be so wrong about ourselves? Now the symphony sits assuredly in the canon of great symphonic works and is soaked with melody and anguish and heartbreak and hope. The slow movement, with a direction from the composer to play in a free, singing style, opens with a set of chords in the lower strings. The violas ostensibly have the tune but it is a rum type of tune, just the top line of chords, which slip from the primordial swamp and eke themselves into a thin slice of sunlight, stretching out a hand towards the major, optimistic key.

And then the horn enters. It is a moment to gasp at humankind's ability to create perfection, both in composition and playing: that Tchaikovsky conceived of this simple tune, so simple, so elegant, so resolute, and that he chose to give the first statement of the tune to the horn, to present the heart of the melody as stalwart and kind. It is a falling scale of easy steps, never reaching too far and always staying within that magic part of the horn, the middle register. The cash register.

As I work on my elevators, I dream of one day making a sound like Peter, or Stefan Dohr, or the Czech soloist Radek Baborák, but there's something that's not flowing, some energy I'm missing. My elevators need maintenance.

One morning I'm doing a workout with Greg, my next-door neighbour. Dr Greg Rowsell is a highly qualified exercise physiologist who has worked with national-level athletes and Olympians, so he has a more basic task with nerdy musician me. We have been doing some work on the deep core, to allow the body to activate in its most natural way. The concepts, from Tim Anderson's *The Becoming Bulletproof Project*, defer to how babies develop movement, and how we can go back to those movements to relearn connections we have lost in our adult lives of sitting, sitting, sitting.

We go on our hands and knees and do head nods, rock backwards and forwards, then roll over and up to a sitting position. It sounds so basic a child could do it, but I've felt my body gain strength without going to the gym once. And I know that with his genius body awareness, Greg's exercises can help me with my horn. Hmm. That came out funny. Anyway, at one point I comment that one side of my body is feeling weaker than the other while doing an exercise, so Greg gets me to lie on my back. I'm wondering why I didn't commit to exercise years ago if it's always this simple, but then Greg asks me to breathe in three different ways, starting with either the belly, the ribs or the upper chest. When we return to the exercise and I keep the strength of the diaphragm in the intercostal muscles of the ribs, I feel like superman. Well, superman in his middle fifties.

'Go and get your horn, Ed. Let's see what happens!'

I race upstairs and return with my horn, loving the mixture of muscle and music.

'Okay, play those exercises I hear you doing in the morning ...'

I breathe in with my ribs activated and set off on one of my elevators, from C through to E, G, B flat, C, D, E – oh my gosh. This is amazing! My elevators, which frequently get stuck at the seventh floor on the B flat (that's the seventh note from the bottom), are now an express lift to the higher floors. All from properly turning on my diaphragm and reminding, allowing, my body to work as it was designed. I then realise Peter has been talking about my ribs for weeks, but I wasn't ready to hear it.

Knowledge of one thing can help another, even if they seem unconnected. One time, a quartet coach told my quartet to watch a circus to improve our playing of Bartók. I don't know how, but it did. Another teacher would present photographs of leaves and trees to show their organic shape and natural balance, as we shaped a phrase in a Haydn quartet. And another teacher, Chris Rowland, would make me jump up and down on the spot for no apparent reason, but it helped my playing become more vibrant and essential.

But knowledge does not always transfer immediately to ability. Some things click straightaway while others take many sleeps to assimilate. And we do not hear advice if we are not ready to listen; we may think we are listening but the time or the vibration isn't right. Sometimes an upside-down approach is best. Reverse-engineering a problem, asking ourselves what we want to do then finding out what we need to do to achieve it offers us a new bearing, and events can unfold naturally rather than being forced.

When my dad was a teenager he wanted to join the merchant navy. To do that he needed to be in the Sea Scouts. To be in the Sea Scouts you needed your own boots. His family couldn't afford boots, but you were given free boots if you joined the army cadets. So Dad joined the army cadets, received his free boots, with those boots joined the Sea Scouts, and then he joined the merchant navy.

We must always ask: how can it get any better than this? And what can we change to allow that to happen? Do we need to do our practice, lie down on the floor and breathe, or watch a circus?

My 'high' C is feeling more middle of the music mountain, and I am extending up to a D and even, if the wind is going in the right direction, an E. What goes up must come down, and my bottom is starting to fill out nicely, thanks to Charlie's cousin Jan's fruitcake. My horn bottom is growing as well, thanks for asking.

Up to now I have been playing on one of Peter's student horns. It's easily good enough for me, with my 53-year-old student sound, but my mum sends all her children a surprising and welcome message that she would like to give us each two thousand British pounds.

'Oooh,' I think. 'Perfect! I can buy a horn!'

I tell Peter and he says, 'That's a perfect amount for a horn!'

He puts the word out among his students and colleagues and within days comes back with an instrument. I go over to his house to meet my new brassy friend. One of Peter's tertiary students has bought a new Alexander horn (the Stradivarius of the horn world, but you don't have to befriend a millionaire to play on one), so she is selling her old horn, a Yamaha 667V. I open the case and there she is, unlacquered (it can give a softer sound) and lying snug in red velvet.

'Go on, have a play!' Peter invites me, and I pick her up. I play an elevator and immediately, even with my beginner playing, the sound is more vibrant and complex. And so much easier.

'Take the horn home and see how you go for the next few days.'

But I already know the answer. Yes, and I name her Anna, after my mum.

I have been playing the viola for so many years that all my knowledge of how to play, and ability to play, has come gradually and often organically. Just as the horn is not an instrument to learn quickly, the viola is also an instrument that takes time to enter its own heart, its own sound, its own character. Violin and viola are similar in technique and violinists will often play the viola as well, but I'm a little sceptical of these players. You need to live the life of a viola player for a long time to fully comprehend the sphere of the viola player.

The viola has such modesty. With its reasonable, human-like voice it plays the inner workings of quartets and symphonies, quietly supporting the main tune, relentlessly driving the pulse, doing the behind-the-scenes work so that others might shine. It sings a short melody full of intangible emotion, somewhere between sadness and resignation, and it reveals the subtle charisma that is its unique beauty. I love the viola's weight, its mutability, its clarity and its mystery. It is my true voice.

Attaining knowledge of this elusive instrument takes time and doing. You cannot learn how to play the viola from a book alone; you need to sit with it, feel its weight with your shoulders, feel its vibrations with your fingers, feel its sonority with your heart. As you ask yourself what you want from the instrument, you are really asking what you want from yourself. And to give yourself the best foundation to play, you must be honest with yourself: what is your true state of mind? What is your basic sound? What do you need to improve, what are your strengths, what do you fear? Only then can you practise properly, with truth.

A long time ago I played in a student quartet. We won a few scholarships and a place to study with the Amadeus Quartet at the Royal Academy of Music in London. Before we went we had a lesson with one of the gurus of quartet playing in England, Sidney Griller. Professor Griller had taught some of the best British quartets, including the Fitzwilliam and the Lindsay. He was a Wayne Bennett of music coaching: that unknowable spark of inspiration, and much easier to understand.

We went around to Professor Griller's house in London and played a Haydn quartet for him. There was a tricky passage for viola that I had not practised properly, because I had not been honest with myself. I always skimmed over it, hoping it would get better on its own, when what I should have done is played with a metronome at the slowest speed I needed to play everything correctly and comfortably, and built up the speed from there. Then and only then can you progress comfortably and safely and confidently, if you have been honest from the beginning.

The Haydn did not go well. I fudged my way through the tricky passage and at the end Professor Griller grilled me with his kind eyes and said, 'That viola part. You need to practise it. Properly.'

I vowed to never allow that to happen again. Through music I had learnt the hard necessity of thoroughness, the undeniable fact that every single note needed to be held inside myself as safely and closely as I would hold a baby. If I wanted to develop beauty in anything, the only way was through preparation. In the perfect words of Richard Gill, 'The difference between an amateur player and a professional player is the amateur player practises a piece until they get it right; a professional player practises a piece until they can't get it wrong.'

———————————

Claudia is in the middle of her viola lesson, and we are looking at the bourrée from Bach's Cello Suite No. 3. This is a dance, and in dances, as in virtually all music, we need a steady rhythm. Actually, we need a steady pulse. Rhythm is what happens inside the pulse; the rhythm can change, but the pulse needs to remain strong and steadfast. Reliable, while still sounding human and not mechanical. Some players swear by practising with a metronome – a device (or app on your phone) that you can set to tick at different speeds – while other players decry metronomes, saying they are unnatural and that our pulse should be allowed to develop organically and not be fettered by a machine. I fall between the two extremes: I can be lazy and so tend to not use a metronome, but my episode with Professor Griller showed me that I really *need* to use one. So that is the habit I am helping my students to develop, to see the metronome as their best friend. It tells you the things you need to know but don't necessarily want to hear. Like, your pulse needs attention.

Claudia began her musical life with the violin, but I persuaded her onto the viola when she was ten. There was something about Claudia that made me think she might like the viola better: her intelligent, subtle outlook on life, her ability to see many layers of meaning in words, and her excellent sense of humour. You need to have that to deal with all the viola jokes. Claudia was a pretty good violinist, but she is an excellent viola player. She has already developed a true viola sound – slightly melancholic, silver and kind. She has just begun learning the bourrée, and as she plays, the pulse of the dance starts to become a little wayward. It's easy to do because the music is hard technically, so we slow down a little and feel the music as an organic, breathing being. Where is the strongest beat, and how does it move to the next beat most naturally? What is the natural order of the music? Where does it want to go, and how?

One of the invitations to string playing is to cross strings very quickly and clearly, but to do that, and keep the pulse stable, is a challenge. In this dance there are lots of string crossings, and that's why the pulse can waver. When I hear this happening, with any student, it feels like the horizon is moving as well as the sea, and any steadiness is lost. A steady pulse is our horizon, our focus, our anchor. We can go up and down as much as we want with the rhythm within the pulse, but the steady, predictable pulse stops us losing our bearings. If we do what we want, with no predictability to our pulse, the music becomes meaningless and fickle. Our pulse is our natural order, and everything must have that. Everything does have that.

But the pulse of the music needs to allow the music to prosper. Too slow and a piece can drag. Imagine *Happy Birthday to You* at a very, very slow pace – the celebration would be lost. Like a cyclist high up the banking in a velodrome, a certain momentum is necessary. But too fast and the music loses its elegance and space. Now imagine Elton John's *Candle in the Wind* – the candle couldn't even be lit if the wind were gale-force. Each piece, each person, has their own natural speed and pulse; we only need to find what that pulse is and then accept it.

After all this work, Claudia plays the piece through one last time and she's got it. The music skips and sashays through to the end, the technical challenges hardly noticed now in the joy of the dance.

———————

There was no joy of the dance for my poor mother. Anna was driven to desperation by the challenge of bringing up four children on her own, and sometimes that desperation would turn into terror for us. One evening we were all told, one by lonely one, what our faults were. My main failing, at the age of eight, was that I was too slow – too slow to walk, too slow to get dressed, too slow to be. It took many years to accept myself and my tendency to do things slowly. Now, whenever I see a student take their time over something, I make sure I praise them for being thoughtful.

It's much harder to play slow music than to play fast music, something I found out with Shostakovich. Chris Rowland, my quartet teacher at the Royal Northern College of Music in Manchester, was the founding first violin in the Fitzwilliam Quartet; the quartet became friends with Shostakovich in the 1970s and gave the Western premieres of his last three string quartets. There is a heft, an inevitability about the Fitzwilliams' playing that suits Shostakovich's music, and much of that heft came from the viola player, Alan George. As my quartet played a slow movement, Chris would tell us stories of the Fitzwilliam Quartet trying to create the right tread for a desperately leaden piece of Shostakovich, and Chris said it was all down to the viola player: Alan George would be in the middle, resolute, immovable, a piece of imploded star with the weight of his pulse.

One.

Two.

Three.

Four.

An enormous abyss between each beat, so big you would want to fill it and arrive at the next beat too early, but Alan George had grown up around marching bands, bands that often play very, very slowly. Between each beat, Alan George had the tenacity to wait.

A beat is time, but what do you do with that time? How do you wait? I was discussing this question with Ben, one of my adult students, just today. He is learning how to change strings without changing the direction of his bow. It's called slurring, and it takes a certain amount of planning and momentum. I put on the metronome and ask Ben to play with it. The first time through is understandably a bit wobbly, but then we try a new idea: splitting the time, the beat, into two, so although Ben is playing at the same speed, inside his head he is counting two beats instead of just one. It's called subdividing, and it means the endless time between slow beats, time when you might lose momentum and want to go faster, that time is now filled mentally, which allows you to relax into the slow pulse. The subdivision is not heard, but you can feel it as a listener because the phrase goes directly to its destiny.

But if we need to change a speed, if we need to change ourselves or others, how do we do it? How do we move faster or slower and not break apart through stress?

There's a beginner piece by Dr Suzuki called *Perpetual Motion*. It's a lot of fun and is used to develop co-ordination between the two sides of the body and fast string crossings. I play 'follow the leader' with my students in this piece to help them develop listening, but also to awaken the desire in them to be with another player not just in space but in spirit. If you share a common goal and are fully aware of other musicians, you can meld your playing together and become more than the sum of your parts. My student and I start off at a regular speed, then I take the lead and we become faster or slower, the change always gradual. If I make sudden changes we fall apart, but if the change is measured, we can reach breakneck speeds and the student comes away exhilarated and wanting more. More speed, less speed, more control, more confidence, more satisfaction, more practice. Gradual change creates a virtuous circle.

———————————

I open the case and lift my viola from its blue velvet. I have had this instrument since 1994, when I was playing with the Hong Kong Philharmonic, and it feels now like a fifth limb of my body. The viola was made by Martin Hilsden in Oxford in 1992, so it's coming up to its thirtieth birthday. A baby still, for a string instrument, and sometimes I think of the years, centuries, this instrument has ahead of it, and how crucial my playing is for its early development. One of the reasons certain instruments sound better than others, beyond the quality of their make, is that they have been used by excellent players. Think of it like a body – if you sit on the couch all day, your muscles will likely not be as well developed as if you walk ten kilometres a day and lift weights. When a string instrument is played well, much is asked of it – volume, subtlety, variety, responsiveness. The more that is asked of it, the more it can offer. So I try to ask more of my viola each time I play it, and each time, like Zoe Knighton with her cello, I try to find where my sound lies. And as I have done that over the years, I have found where my inner sound lies.

To play an instrument is to have an expansion of your body. Not an addition or an addendum but an augmentation. My hand flows into my bow, stroking and stimulating the strings, and my shoulder flows into my viola, becoming a magnificent superhero body, wide and bold and able to produce an infinitude of sound.

As the viola has grown into me, and I into it, I have felt the shifts in proprioception within myself. From the age of twelve I have played the viola sometimes for eight hours a day, so by the time I was thirty-three and realised I was transgender, I had developed a singular awareness of my body, noticing the tiniest changes through playing. That awareness gave, and continues to give, a depth and sureness to my awareness of being transgender.

For me, one of the chasms of transgender horror was my body not feeling as I knew it was meant to feel. When I moved through space, it didn't match how I moved in my head. The disconnection was only bearable when I played music, but playing music made me more and more aware. Music became my haven and my hell. In the last few years before I began my transition I stopped playing altogether, unable to bear the transparency of it all. Playing music was too honest for me when I was determined to lie to myself. Yet it was the only time I felt any hope or sense of place, or my body held any value. So, logically, when I stopped playing music or even teaching for a few years in my forties, my body lost its meaning and value. No wonder I ruptured.

When you play an instrument, even in your first lesson, you receive instant feedback. You might imagine it's mostly your hearing that gives you information, but it's much more complex than that. Taste is the only sense to not be utilised, although I have seen some young boys lick their cellos, so I wouldn't want to rule it out completely.

As you play with your bow, through your fingers, arm and all the way to your torso, you feel the weight of the bow on the string, the speed, the contact, the spring of the string supporting the bow. Over time the slightest change in any of these feels monumental. You see the angles of your bow hair and you smell the rosin as it sticks to the strings.

And through the fingers of your left hand, as they bring the strings down to the fingerboard to change the pitches, you feel a constant tingle as the strings pick up the sympathetic vibrations of the whole instrument. Through your shoulders you feel the binding and co-ordination of both arms, and you enrol the large muscles of your back, your wing muscles, as the spirit of your sound. Your core is strong and supple all the way down through your loose hips to your feet, rooted into the earth. You feel gravity helping you, and ultimately playing becomes an infinite loop of your body, from left hand through instrument to right hand, from the back to the front, from fingertips to toes, swirling around again and again, and the earth supporting you and bringing your bow and fingers to the string. Playing an instrument, any instrument, is an orgy of sensation.

In the final stanza of 'The Dry Salvages', the third of T.S. Eliot's 'Four Quartets', Eliot writes:

> *For most of us, there is only the unattended*
> *Moment, the moment in and out of time,*
> *The distraction fit, lost in a shaft of sunlight,*
> *The wild thyme unseen, or the winter lightning*
> *Or the waterfall, or music heard so deeply*
> *That it is not heard at all, but you are the music*
> *While the music lasts.*

Strangely, I had seen this quote painted on an electricity box beside the freeway in Brisbane. As some phrases do, it buried itself, no, sowed itself in my mind until I was ready to listen.

I understand now. I understand that with music, we have in our own hands the ability to step beyond time, to the eternal now.

I have been taking testosterone for five years. Every ten weeks I go to my doctor and have a large needle full of Swiss-made testosterone injected into my butt. Dr Bearman is the best doctor ever and I hardly feel a thing, but the things I feel because of that injection, they are life-saving. I obsessed for years about transitioning, finding every single website, video, book and forum about what it is to transition. As I began my own transition, the obsession refined to reflection – reflection on how I was to make the most of my new life, my new world, my new being. And from reflection I now feel a comprehensive amalgamation.

Through music, I have learnt how to learn. I have learnt that curiosity, examination, attention, honesty and process are the utensils for our lives. And with them, we can learn anything.

I have learnt that practice is my prayer. With practice we obsess, we reflect, we amalgamate. With practice, we can look inside and find our rhythm, our sound, our pulse. And we can trust in it to work, always.

With practice, we know how to know ourselves.

C:

RESILIENCE

Music exists for the
purpose of growing an
admirable heart.

DR SHINICHI SUZUKI

———————————

Don't be afraid to give up.

J.E.G. AYRES

MAX IS TEN. Strong. A climber, an adventurer, a boy of action, with wide hands and few words.

Max came for lessons with me when he was eight. He had been learning in a group class at school, but he and his parents felt he needed more individual attention, so they called me up and we started to learn together. I say 'learn together' because in the healthiest lesson settings, I will learn as much as my students – it might not be how to better read music, but it may well be how to better read people.

Max had lessons with me for a couple of terms but it just wasn't working. For either of us. He was taciturn and seemed to viscerally hate his lessons, and I was flailing around, searching for Max's learning style – trying different pieces, talking a lot, not talking at all, asking questions, making statements, learning with the written music, learning by ear – but nothing seemed to stick. I was failing Max and I felt guilty. It didn't come as a surprise when Max's mum called me and said Max would not continue lessons the next term. I felt guilty, but I also felt some relief. Then I felt guilty at feeling relieved. I tried to make excuses for myself – maybe it just wasn't the right instrument for Max, or maybe he didn't like music at all – but anyway, now I didn't have to worry about him and I could teach students who communicated more readily and seemed to enjoy playing more.

How wrong I was. As the next term started and I took on a new, obviously keen, student to fill Max's space, I missed Max. I couldn't help feeling there had been an opportunity lost, and that I needed to learn from the experience. I reread Dr Suzuki's *Nurtured by Love* and realised if I had taught Max from a position of love, it would not have mattered how much he improved. Love will always provide the right compass bearing.

And so I moved on and filled my heart with love for my students, no matter the sound of the playing, their sometimes indiscriminate rhythms, or their occasional disregard for the beauties of music.

And then, at the beginning of the following year, a message from Max. Well, from his mum.

Hi, Ed – Max wondered if you had space to teach him again? He's been thinking about it and would like to give the cello another go.

Oh, wow. This from a boy who was by now only nine, and he had had the maturity and self-reflection to think, 'That decision wasn't made in the best frame of mind; I will reconsider.'

How many of us in adulthood have shown such excellent character? I replied immediately and said, 'Yes, please', shuffled a few students around and Max started to come again for lessons on Fridays.

In those six months, Max had opened and relaxed. From my position of now teaching only with love, I had done the same. I didn't try any special tactic or plan, I simply responded to how Max was on the day. Each week he opened more, and we chatted about climbing and mountain biking, and how high he had jumped on his bike and how far he had run to school. True, it sometimes took a third of the lesson before we played any music, but building the shelter of trust and joy was worth it. His cello playing became freer and happier, and he started to learn with fresh ease and joy. Max looked me more in the eye and even started to volunteer information about his day without me asking. Then, one lesson, he looked sideways at me, a tiny smile hovering beside his mouth.

'Ed, look at this!'

He took his mum's phone and showed me a three-minute stop-motion animation he had made with Lego for school. It was a story about a marine vet who is eaten by his patient, a hammerhead shark. Max had written the story, shot the footage, done the editing, and composed and recorded the music. He played the score for me right there, a grumbling plaint on the low strings to illustrate the shark and the grim death in his film. I recorded the music, wrote it out on my computer and gave the sheet music to Max in his next lesson.

Max had rightly been very pleased with his film, and when he saw his composition written out with a title page and composer credit, his freckly face lit up.

'Thank you, Ed,' he said simply, and Max put the music carefully away in his folder.

Max brings a composition to most lessons now. He promises not to forget me when he receives his Oscar for best original film score.

Many years ago, my dad gave me some useful advice. I was planning to cycle from England to Hong Kong, and I went to see him before I left. Dad told me a story of a friend of his who had planned to sail around the world. The friend had spent months and months, and tens of thousands of dollars, preparing. There was a huge media fuss about the adventure (even before the internet); the expectation and demand for vicarious stimulation from all around him was heavy. He left on the due date to great fanfare and amazement at the bravery of the man, his sense of adventure and determination. On the second day, already far out to sea, the sailor turned his boat around and headed home. He had had the character to admit that he had made the wrong decision. He had had the character to not be afraid to give up.

When Dad told me this story, it freed something in me. I completed my trip but always felt that if I wanted to, I could have stopped. I could have given up. And the same with Max. He had had the integrity to give up, knowing it wasn't the right path for him, but he had gone even further, changing his mind and trusting himself. So I may have been teaching Max since he was eight, but really, Max has been teaching me since I was fifty-one.

———————————

Playing and learning music requires a continual border crossing between the language of our physical world and the language of music. Musicians are constantly making that journey and live perpetually in a bilingual world. Or is it a parallel universe?

Living across two worlds means, by convenience, you end up living close to the border, in a liminal space where the two blend and the border crossing is hardly noticed. Still, no matter how close to the border you live, to speak the new language of music you must let go a little of your old language of words and use a different part of your brain, the part that gives you access to everything.

A musician takes dots on a page, and, often among a hundred other musicians, interprets those dots within a millisecond of time, to play them with exact articulation, length, pitch, dynamic and shape. We do that with a level of precision only an Olympic athlete would come close to understanding.

What happens when we speak another language? To do it convincingly we leave our home, our mother tongue, our familiarity behind and stand fully in the new world. For a musician to study, interpret and comprehend a piece of music, we must be naked inside it. Any trace of our old world is as useless to musicians as an old school friend is to an undercover spy. We become the music and accept whatever it makes of us, and the time it takes from us.

But there are similarities between music and our spoken, wordy language. When I am speaking English, I am not necessarily conscious of the articulation of my speech, or how long I give a certain vowel, or the stress of a syllable. But if I had not learnt English as my mother tongue, it may be that some of those emphases would be different. Hos-*pit*-al. In-*gen*-uity. Swapping a V for a W, or an absent H. Musicians consider all these things too, so when a musician plays, they must enunciate as clearly as they do in their mother tongue.

A musician is an orator, an oracle, an actor, a poet, a philosopher, a mathematician, a psychologist, an architect, an alchemist.

Musicians become adept at crossing the boundary from the word sphere to the sound sphere, and once we are there, crossing boundaries of time, style, form and meaning. In a single concert a player can leap from the eighteenth century and a small town in Austria, to Soviet Russia and the misery of the Second World War, and on to a bucolic view of England and willows in the early twentieth century. A musician in an orchestra can leap from playing full pelt with their hundred colleagues and shaking the earth, to teetering solo on a ledge, high above the hall. No wonder musicians travel so easily to different countries and become so flexible with our work. Besides, here in Australia, very few permanent jobs come up, apart from teaching.

Q: 'What's the first thing a musician says when
   they are at work?'
A: 'Would you like fries with that?'

To support myself I have been a cleaner, a fishmonger, a cleaner again, a bartender, a kitchenhand, a deli assistant (I was fired for eating the sandwiches) and a larder chef. Nothing at music college prepared me for any of it, but everything I learnt at music college prepared me for it. Just as every musician is equally important in the orchestra, I learnt that every job in society was important. Viola players often have very, very repetitive parts, especially in waltzes, so I was already mentally prepared for cleaning thousands of dishes in a café in St Kilda. Musicians work unsocial hours, so I was ready to be a larder chef. Musicians need to sell their music to the audience, so I was made to be a fishmonger and sell day-old fish. It was sometimes easier than selling Schubert to schoolchildren.

Sometimes I see my first instrument, the viola, as a border instrument. Years ago I wrote a paper called 'The Viola: A small cello, a big violin, or just a joke?' The viola didn't seem to belong. Our parts in symphonies didn't seem to make much difference, and we were either playing with the second violins and trying to find melody in accompaniment, excitement in a single note, or we were playing with the cellos and feeling inadequate compared with their hero sound. The viola is always visiting other instruments' countries, because our own is small and lacking in resources. We play transcriptions of pieces originally for violin or cello, and our technical books are adapted from violin. It is as if viola players are always on temporary visas in the land of music.

What changed then, for me? A realisation that being on the border between instruments was an incredibly powerful place to be. Because our own repertoire is a little small, we need to look elsewhere for fulfilment, so we take the best bits of repertoire from any instrument and play the music with our own indescribable beauty. I often hear people say the violin is humanity's soul and the cello is humanity's voice, so what is the viola? I believe the viola is the sound of humanity's resilience.

Shostakovich's final piece was for viola, and he must have known it would be his last. In the last of the three movements of his viola sonata, Shostakovich uses excerpts from Beethoven's *Moonlight Sonata*, with the dotted rhythm invoking the funeral march, and quotes from all fifteen of his own symphonies. It is as if we are being taken year by year, piece by piece, challenge by horror by disappointment by terror, through Shostakovich's existence. This was not the act of a man who thought there would be more life after this. He knew it was his final work and he chose the viola as his final voice.

So much of Shostakovich's music is angry, so much is tragic, so much is grimly happy, but this piece reaches beyond any such worldly emotion. The tone of the piece means we must let go, and the quality of the viola, that quality of depth without sinking, height without vertigo, means the viola is the kindest of instruments to help us. With his viola sonata, Shostakovich is saying, 'It is enough – I have done what I could, and this piece is my last will and testament.'

————————

Musicians leave much behind. We must, to be light enough to travel. We leave behind friends and homes and audiences and teachers and partners, all so we can give concerts for people we don't know, and express emotions on stage only our closest friends should ever see. So when I finally, after fifteen years, accepted I needed to transition, that I needed to leave behind my female body, I knew I had the strength to go through with it, and the flexibility and creativity for it to also be joyous. Yes, like a difficult performance I know I have prepared for properly, I dared dream of joy.

I returned to Australia from Kabul in 2016 and started taking testosterone on 21 July – my manniversary. For the next few months I wrote my book *Danger Music* and began the task of officially changing my name and gender.

As I contacted the tax office, the passport office, the motorbike insurance office, the Medicare office, the bank, the driving licence office, the superannuation office, the Working with Children Check office, a surprising fact was revealed to me: at every single place I visited, someone had a friend/cousin/child/parent who was also transitioning. Crikey, it began to feel almost, dare I say it, run of the mill. Not one single person batted an eyelid when I told them. After all those years of thinking it would be too hard, I managed to complete my official gender and name changing in a couple of days. With the correct letter from my doctor, it was no more emotional than updating my credit card details. One woman even said, 'Oh, don't worry, honey – we get you folks in here all the time!'

Apart from one afternoon in the post office.

I had applied to change the gender on my passport and went to the local post office with my forms. The first woman who helped me was hilarious; we went over the forms and she told me how brave she thought I was, and it was a delightful experience. I had to come back a few days later with more details and saw a different woman. Younger, tougher. When I presented the same forms she said in a very loud voice, in front of a dozen people, 'Look, are you a man or a woman? What does it say on your birth certificate? If it says you're a woman, that's what you are.'

I explained that I had a letter from my doctor, a psychiatrist report, everything I needed to change my gender. The worker snatched the letter from me and pointed out I had forgotten my passport photos. I had to go home to collect them, then return.

Back at home I explained to Charlie what had happened.

'You need to say something. If she says that to you and you don't speak up, she'll carry on doing it to everyone.'

I knew Charlie was right, but I also knew that rage wouldn't work. When I returned I put on my best calm radio voice and spoke very politely. It felt like a viola performance – persuasive, welcoming, unexpected. I couldn't afford to be nervous.

'Perhaps you might like to think about how you would approach this situation differently in the future? I personally don't mind anyone knowing I'm transgender, but there are many people who keep it secret, for their own safety. We get beaten up and killed, you know. Being transgender is tough, and being publicly exposed and embarrassed like that would send many people over the edge. Would you mind just having a think about it?'

The post office worker looked down at the counter, ashamed, resentful. She's avoided my eye ever since.

As 2016 ended, I started to look for work. I was nearly fifty, and I had to begin my life again. Everything I had built over the last twelve years in Australia was gone; I didn't even have my name anymore. Because of the desperation my gender dysphoria had punched me with, I had resigned from the ABC and had no hope of returning. Sure, I had changed my legal gender with no problems, but what would it be like with work? I was burdened with fear that I wouldn't be allowed to teach – no-one would want a transgender person at their school or close to their child. I would have to develop a new career like cooking or gardening. I had rebuilt my life when I immigrated to Australia, and if I needed to, I would do it again. But this time was harder. I lay awake at night imagining the different embodiments of failure, shame and embarrassment that were sure to befall me, a transgender person.

I applied for a few cello teaching jobs, one in a Christian college where I didn't even get an interview and one at a private girls school near Brisbane. I was given an interview, and I revelled in putting on a suit and tie rather than a Laura Ashley dress. Testosterone was beginning to change my physical appearance: hair had moved from the top of my skull to the bottom, my shoulders were filling out, and, most importantly for me, my voice had dropped considerably. If you didn't know I was transgender, you wouldn't really be able to tell.

I had the interview and the next day was offered the job, a part-time position with room for expansion teaching cello to junior and senior girls. Great, I thought. This is going to be a breeze after Afghanistan. Order, calm, predictability, no bombs. I was asked to show copies of my qualifications, so I let the school know the certificates were in my old name of Emma, but I could also send them a copy of my name change certificate.

Silence.

I didn't hear from the school for five days. Of course, I knew what was happening. They had offered me the job, in writing, and now they were committed to employing a transgender man at a girls school, and who knew what the parents might think and how many girls would be taken out of school or what scandal would ensue? To them, I was a big problem.

I emailed the school and asked if there was, indeed, a problem. No, no, they replied, just a few administrative hurdles, then they would send me the contract. I decided I would take my chances elsewhere and let them know I wouldn't be taking the job. I could hear their sigh of relief over email. I later found out the school had a shocking reputation and that I had dodged a bullet of dysfunction.

I still had to find work, though, and decided to apply for big toughie jobs.

Ferry deckhand.

Not even a response.

Qantas baggage handler.

No. Thanks for the letter, though, Qantas. At least you replied.

Bakery delivery driver.

No, but I did get to eat some nice buns in my bakery delivery driver trial.

Just before the next school year started, I found out about a teaching job at another private school. They were desperate to find a cello teacher and wanted to interview me straightaway.

Charlie and I decided to make a day of it, I put my suit on again and we drove to the school.

The school grounds could not have been more in contrast with the school I had taught at in Kabul. Instead of steel gates and a dusty courtyard without a single blade of grass there was pristine fencing and acres of lawn. Instead of a single low building with filthy windows there were countless buildings, each of which could have been a stately home. And instead of soldiers with AK47s there were groundskeepers with peaceful hoes.

I headed to the school office. It was a banal interview, just going through my CV, until a surprising statement came. The school had somehow found out about my medical background and had referred my appointment to the school board to check they approved of employing a transgender man. It got worse. I was told the school had written to parents of the cello students to ask if they approved of me, a transgender man, teaching their children. I was also told where I should use the bathroom: not the men's, as was my right, but the disabled toilet.

I was stunned into submission. I was also forced into submission by my bank balance. It was the beginning of the year, I had applied for many jobs, and this was the only one I had a chance of getting. The only thing I needed to do was to swallow my pride, and my legal rights.

I swallowed.

———————————————

My horn playing has been advancing in a 'two steps forward, one and a half steps back' kind of way, which I have found difficult to accept, although the cacophony of animal noises coming from my music room seems to be confusing the neighbours a little less and they (the neighbours, not the animals) have started to move back into the area.

Anna, my new horn, and I are getting to know each other a little better. We have moved past the 'How do you do?' phase to me now sticking my hand up her bottom. Sticking your hand up a horn's bottom, or bell, changes the pitch and the quality of sound, so this is an important step.

Getting to know a horn, as with a baby, involves finding the best way to get rid of excess fluid. For some horns, you need to spin them around until the condensation (oh, okay, there's a bit of spit in there as well) comes out, or you can jiggle the valves in a certain way and empty any liquid from the crooks. Anna, like a true lady, likes to be spun around, so I play a few elevators, twirl her like a dance partner and carry on.

It is so important to have support when anyone starts something new. A long time ago, I saw a father dismiss his daughter with the words, 'I don't know why you're bothering to play – you always sound as bad as you did in the first lesson.' The daughter, despite my efforts, gave up the next term. But Charlie is the perfect supportive partner. Like a sports commentator, I call out my latest achievement from the music room: a new note! A bigger sound! The dog doesn't want to escape!

Each time, Charlie replies with, 'That's great, Eadric, keep practising.' And I know she means it. She also calls me a big, hairy brute, which is about the best thing you can say to a trans bloke.

The feedback we receive as new musicians is beyond important. It forms the kernel of how we feel about our playing, now and into our future. If a student is constantly told they are making a 'bad' sound, that they are playing the wrong notes, that their rhythm and pulse is erratic, a little part of those students will die every time they play because they will start to think they are not good enough. And if you are not good enough at one thing, well, why would you be good enough at anything? Why would you bother trying at all? This holds true for students of any age and any level. Thank heavens the days are gone of music teachers with rulers to rap the knuckles of wayward fingers, but damaging feedback doesn't have to come from a teacher. It can be an older sibling telling you to shut up, they want to listen to their music. Or it can be from an uncle, laughing at the way you look when you play. Or it can be from a parent, complaining how much it costs and how much time it takes and is it really worth it? Are you really worth it?

My practice when I was young was smothered by stress. My mum enforced regular practice (good) but was unrelenting in her enforcement (bad). The five of us lived in a small house, so any practice was heard by everyone. This was before the days of individual phones and music and headphones, so when I practised, my beginner sound became the dominant one in the house. And this meant certain siblings were constantly telling me to stop practising.

Or practise quieter.

Or better.

Just be better.

My playing became wrapped in a coil of demand, desire and acquiescence. No wonder practice on the viola still doesn't come easily to me. Practice on the horn is much simpler.

I return to Peter for a lesson. We are now having lessons once every two weeks, as this gives me time to assimilate and practise what Peter has given me.

One of the great challenges for me with the horn is that I cannot see the bits of my body that play the instrument. I play the viola with my fingers and arms and back, so I can quickly correct an angle or placement, but I play the horn with my diaphragm and breath and tongue and mouth cavity, so everything must be based on that most ephemeral of senses, feel. Sure, I can see my stomach expanding as I breathe in, and I can check the outer part of my embouchure, but everything else is inside. This makes the importance of Peter's teaching even greater.

After about two months of lessons, Tim in the Queensland Symphony Orchestra casually says to me, 'Ed, you do know Peter is one of the best horn teachers in the world, don't you?' And yet Peter continues to welcome me each fortnight as if I am a great youthful prospect, rather than an ageing viola player who is writing a book and wants to have a bit of a go.

Without prompting, Peter says, 'What I like about teaching you is we can go through the process in detail, and I know you'll do the work.' I admit it – I am putting myself down. When I started the horn, I thought it would be a 'bit of a go', but I have seriously fallen in love with it. And when

I say I do an hour's practice every day, I often do more, then my embouchure collapses on me like a deflated balloon and I have to stop.

So when, after a couple of love-filled, practice-filled months, I am still having problems achieving any stability whatsoever above a middling C, I am a tad frustrated. My attempts at higher notes remind me of cadet soldiers trying to climb a steel wall. Gathering all your force and effort each time, and each time failing and falling back to where you started. In the mud. I mean, I know this is a difficult instrument, but how does anyone get anywhere at all? It seems the more I try, the worse it gets. Some days a dry rasp comes out of my horn, as if she has been dehydrated and is only sticking together because it's more convenient. Other days a loud fart comes out of nowhere (well, definitely from the horn) but I have no idea what I did differently to make her sound so … rude.

I just thank the gods of music that I didn't choose the oboe. Sorry, oboists.

'Ed, you're making it too hard. Digging a ditch is hard, but not difficult. Playing the horn is difficult, but not hard.' Peter smiles, Buddha-like.

Om. There's a metaphor in everything. And in music, especially playing the horn, you don't have to look very hard at all to find one.

Richard Gill once wisely said, 'The time you want to practise the least is the time you need to practise the most.' I have practised in practice rooms (no surprise there), bathrooms (men's and women's, and been thrown out of both), railway carriages (good for your music pulse), bathrooms on railway carriages (not good for your heart pulse), paddocks (the cows like Mahler), cars (best for fast pieces), airports (who lets a viola through security?), garages (better acoustic than the practice room) and gardens (the roses were dead before I got there, honest!). I have practised at 5 a.m., 1 a.m., for eight hours a day, for ten minutes a day and for decades. And for a decade I did not practise. When I started the cello in my thirties, I left the viola behind for ten years to give my hands and heart a chance to transition.

Now I have my viola firmly back in my life and I have just started practising after a week's holiday. I put on my shoulder rest, wind up my bow, apply some rosin, tune my viola and start at the beginning.

I place my bow on the D string, the second string from the top. The D string always feels comfortable, so I start there and play some open strings, feeling my way into the sound, allowing my body to follow where my ears and heart guide me. As the sound starts to flow, I move on to the other strings and play with different speeds of note and bow. Each string demands different angles of bow and elbow height, and modified weight and placement of the bow on the string. And each part of the bow demands a change in weight and angle. At the tip, the far end of the bow from the right hand, I imagine the sound coming from the middle of my back, playing with my wing muscles. This pulls a wider, deeper sound from the viola than if I simply pressed on the string. And the reverse at the bottom of the bow, the heel. There I stroke the viola's strings carefully, like stroking a cat who is a bit tricky. It is easy to break the sound here, to allow too much weight to drop down and suffocate the vibrations.

When I haven't played for a few days I feel like a novice again, which is no bad thing. It allows me to reassess any bad habits and notice where any tension sits. When I practise, in a way every time is like the first time. I try to listen without assumption and with a resistance to going ahead too quickly. I play a slow descending scale and search for the heart of each note, so my viola may vibrate as fully as it is able. Once I feel my fingers are woken up, I play some fast finger exercises and do some shifting, moving my left hand to different positions on the instrument. This is when people often comment, 'Oh my gosh, how do you know where to put your fingers? You don't have any of those line things, like on a guitar.'

Frets. No, we don't have those, although we can start with sticky-tape frets for the first year or two. Where a string player places their left hand is all done by sound and feel and muscle memory; it takes hundreds of thousands of repetitions to have any sense of certainty that you are going where you want to go. Again and again and again. Ten times in a row, I tell my students. If you stuff it up on the tenth time, go back to the beginning. It is effective, but compared with other teachers, this is practice-lite. I heard tales of a Russian cello teacher who had a long comb and a small piece of paper. Practise a shift, get it right, move the paper along one tine. Until the end of the comb. Hmm, maybe I should try it with my kids ...

Belinda Manwaring, my cello teacher, has arranged a concert for her students, and she has also asked me to play the solo part in the Telemann Viola Concerto, with Belinda and her senior students playing the orchestral parts. I haven't played a viola concerto for a very long time; this one is not technically hard, but even so, I need to practise, practise, practise.

Having a deadline of a performance creates a two-headed rush: a desire to practise and a fear of not being 'good enough'. They are opposite and apposite. Of course, if you do the first, you shouldn't have to worry about the second, right? But the more I practise, the more I fear I am not doing enough and will let Belinda down. But I have learnt to ignore my mind and get on with the serious business of playing.

The first time I played the Telemann Viola Concerto, I was fourteen. I was the soloist with the Shropshire Youth Orchestra, playing in a cold school gymnasium beside the Shropshire Hills. I've loved the piece ever since, and I've now played and practised and taught it hundreds of times; it's when you teach a piece that you really know it. As I start the music, after teaching it to Claudia last year, I observe new pathways through the music and hear unexplored patterns and opportunities. Walking the same path over decades, you see new things if you're showing a friend the way.

When musicians practise and perform a piece of music, we are praying at a temple where generations of people have come before us. We are building on a collective love and knowledge. The teacher who first gave me this music, Simon Stace, was in turn taught by his teacher, and they by theirs, all the way back through the generations to Telemann himself. The patina builds and the line is unbroken.

It is 3.20 p.m. on Thursday, which means it is time to pack my cello into my van and drive over to Rosie's house for her lesson. Rosie lives among gum trees and kookaburras (she does live in a house as well), and our cello lesson floats out to the elderly neighbours who stay in on Thursdays to listen. The sound of a lesson, of a young student copying and trying and failing, is the soundtrack to resilience. We try, we fail. We try, we fail a little less. We try, we still fail, but now we can feel where failing ends.

Rosie greets me with a grin, a twirl and a pacy rendition of who did what at school today, and isn't it interesting that some kids in her class don't even know what a cello is, let alone know how to play it?

Rosie has developed a soft bow hold and a naturally fluid and graceful bow arm, which I suspect is from her also learning ballet. She is using all her fingers on the top two strings, the

A and the D, and this means we can now play a true classic of pedagogy: *Twinkle, Twinkle, Little Star.*

Today Rosie and I are working on memory, and we are going to have a picnic.

Learning to play an instrument, and then learning to play a piece from memory, can seem an insurmountable task. When you think of the complexity for pianists learning Liszt by heart, or conductors memorising Bruckner symphonies, surely it's an achievement reserved for the very talented, the very intelligent, the very different from us?

No. We can all do it, we just need to start at the beginning and take a sensible route.

Back to the picnic. *Twinkle* is a perfect piece to memorise because it is a musical sandwich. Sing it with me:

Twinkle, twinkle, little star
　　How I wonder what you are

Up above the world so high
　　Like a diamond in the sky

Twinkle, twinkle, little star
　　How I wonder what you are

As you can hear, the beginning and the end are the same, so they become the bread. The middle tune is repeated, so that becomes your double filling. The academic name is ternary form (ABA), but doesn't sandwich-making sound more appetising?

All you need to do now is decide what kind of sandwich you want.

'I am going to have white bread,' says Rosie. (I agree. This is the stand-out choice for sandwiches.) 'And my filling is going to be … butter and sprinkles!'

We sing the tune, play it loud and excited or quiet and a little sad. I try to confuse Rosie and play a wrong note and she yells in horror. We take it in turns playing either the bread or the filling, then we turn our sandwich inside out and play the filling first. I play half a phrase and Rosie finishes it, then four notes and Rosie the next four, then two and two, until we get down to playing a note each, all the way through. Rosie's mum's challenge is to close her eyes and work out who is playing what. It's a grand musical workout, and by the end, Rosie has memorised her *Twinkle*. Rosie now has many tools to remember the music, and even though this piece is short and simple, the same tools are used for a piece long and elaborate. Rosie has used visualisation, emotion, spatial awareness, proprioception, storytelling, comedy and taste. Oh, and aural memory, for good measure.

But she's done more than memorise a piece of music. Rosie hasn't just repeated someone else's *Twinkle*, she has made the music her own. She has taken her instrument and played with her own intent, phrasing, meaning and sound. Rosie has taken possibly the most important music journey of them all: she has re-created music from her own memory and followed an abstract form as closely as a city map. She has travelled from A to B and back to A, and now she need never get lost.

'To remember is to be free.' This phrase has popped into my head, and I cannot think who said it or why I thought it. It drips away through my head for an afternoon, bothering me.

And then I understand.

Remembering music opens other memories for us, memories that, in some part of us, we have chosen to forget. The sentiment of a piece can unlock the emotions we felt as we listened to it before, and as we remember, we become more aware of our past, and less its hostage. Music is the universal key for opening our memory locker, and when those memories need to be relived to be expunged, music is our warden.

'To remember is to be set free.' Maybe that's better.

The path of the music we've listened to trails behind and in front of us. We can listen to anything we choose: fourteenth-century chant, twentieth-century hip-hop, music of revolution, music of prayer. Silence.

We become our own curators of feeling. By choosing what we listen to, not what our siblings or parents or friends tell us to listen to, we are staking a place just for ourselves. Liam, my eleven-year-old viola student, does this already. Liam refuses to listen to anything other than classical music. Well, he did give Nina Simone a go, for a weekend. Then he went straight back to Bach on Monday. Liam, through music, has a clear perception of who he is.

Few of us are as mature as Liam, especially at the age of eleven. I think I was still watching cartoons and listening to the leftovers of my siblings.

Charlie, my partner, grew up in Brisbane and longed for something different.

'I felt, in my parents' home, incredibly deprived of the music and the culture I craved. When I was a student nurse, with my first pay packet I bought a record player and my first vinyls. There was a record catalogue – you could try out vinyls, and if you didn't like them you just returned them. I would start off with simple things like the Tchaikovsky Violin Concerto.'

Once Charlie had completed her nursing training, she moved to London.

'Here I was, a simple Brisbane girl, going to Covent Garden Opera House in the early seventies. In the flat under mine lived a group of musicians who sang Schubert lieder. I thought they were royalty. One of the big things that came out around then was Vivaldi's *The Four Seasons* by I Musici. I found it connected me to a new group of people who loved classical culture. After I came back to Australia I moved to Java and became immersed in Javanese classical culture. I studied dance, and my friends studied gamelan. The *kratons*, the palaces, had regular shadow puppet plays, so we would go on the full moon, listening late at night. It was so romantic, outside my own white Australian culture. This is an ancient culture; the music of Yogyakarta and Solo is very refined and spiritual, and for me, as an Australian, it was a completely new experience.'

The sounds of early morning magpies float in to the house, as Charlie floats into her past.

'I believe my spiritual studies were heightened by the music. The teachings I received gave a framework for my life – I learnt a new way of thinking and behaving, more in the Buddhist tradition. The music took me out of my culture and allowed me to look at myself, my life, and how I wished to transform it: to be a more refined person spiritually, selfless, and with the understanding that all life is one. With the rituals of our life we create an environment that enhances. You follow the rituals of your meditation and your belief system, and you feel unconditional love.'

Practice, practice, practice.

───────────────

They started at night at 10.30 p.m., precise as a metronome. I would be asleep, and they would shake me awake into a howl of disbelief. Disbelief at the pain I was in. Somebody was driving a nail into my right eye at the same time that someone else was pulling a nail out of the same eye. The only thing I could do was

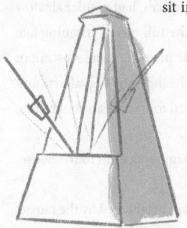 sit in bed and rock myself backwards and forwards until the pain went away. Paracetamol was not even touching the sides of the agony.

At first I thought it was my sinuses, or my teeth. I had had pain like this before in Hong Kong and had to have a root canal. But then I worried it might be my horn playing. I had been very committed to practising over the last month or so, and perhaps something had burst inside my brain? Had I been using too much pressure to play my middling C? There had been a trumpeter at college, Geraint, who had died from an aneurysm. Was this a thing for brass players? Was I going to have to give up? And there was a history of stroke in my family on both sides …

After the headaches started to happen in the early morning as well, I acquiesced and went to the doctor. Dr Leonie asked me very detailed questions.

'When do they start? What does it feel like? Can you feel tingling anywhere else? How long do they last? What is your level of pain between one and ten, where ten is unbearable?'

'Thirteen.'

There were probably more questions, but by now I felt I was beginning to lose my mind, so desperate was I to find out what was wrong so she could *make them stop*. Leonie sent me for a scan, but nothing. Well, apart from the usual things you would expect: brain, spinal cord, etc. I went to the dentist, nothing. Each night I would wake at exactly the same time and I would have nail after nail driven into my cheekbone and my eye, someone would scrape it around in an indescribable spot close to my brain and slowly pull it out again. I could only rock myself, walk like a zombie, punch myself on my leg to divert the pain somewhere else, and eventually scream in horror. After two weeks I went back to Leonie.

'Leave it with me, I'll call you tomorrow.'

Leonie called the next day.

'Okay, I have good news and bad news. Which do you want first?'

Always the bad news. End on a high.

'Bad news: you have something called cluster headaches, and there is no cure. The giveaway is the regularity of the timing, and that they are on one side of your face. And the good news: you are not going to die from them, they come in groups, hence the name clusters, and they will go away … sometime. Probably in a few weeks.'

Sure, I wouldn't die from them, but as they were happening, I felt like I wanted to.

Cluster headaches have been described as the worst pain humans experience, apart from childbirth. No-one knows why they happen, apart from some connection with the hypothalamus. The clusters can happen at any time, usually last for a few weeks, then go away for a year or so, but some desperately unlucky people have them chronically. When you are in the middle of a cluster they can be triggered by alcohol, so I gave up my nightly whisky and resigned myself to rocking and punching and screaming for the foreseeable future.

Leonie prescribed some medication, rizatriptan, which would hopefully take the edge off the headaches. It seemed to work, but I was having to take a pill every night, and the pills were very expensive. Charlie and I went away to the beach for a few days to try to relax and I had to bring a bigger bag to accommodate my new extravagantly packaged drug habit. This was my first experience of being utterly dependent on a drug to live with any confidence and optimism. But then I realised that without testosterone I wouldn't be able to live a full life – without testosterone I wouldn't be alive at all, not in any meaningful way. So take your pill, be grateful you can afford it, be grateful you live in a country where most of the cost is paid for by taxes, and accept this is your life, for now.

As my head was colonised by pain, or waiting for the pain, I yearned for something to happen between my ears that didn't make me shudder. I kept practising the horn, careful not to overdo the higher notes, and rested my mind with quieter music: de Hartmann and his arrangements of the folk music notated by Gurdjieff, Sculthorpe and his *Little Passacaglia*, some Rameau and then, an astonishing new discovery for me, Górecki and his third string quartet.

Henryk Górecki is best known for his *Symphony of Sorrowful Songs*, a work that brought him huge commercial success fifteen years after its composition. If you have not listened to it yet, please give yourself a present and listen to it this evening, with the lights dimmed. And pour yourself a whisky if you don't have a cluster headache. I had heard this symphony many times, played it in Hong Kong and written about it in my book *Cadence*, but I was curious what else this Polish composer had to offer. Surely, with the minimalism and lamenting balm of the symphony, he would have something else to help my damaged head.

Górecki's third quartet was commissioned by the Kronos Quartet in the early 1990s, but it took Górecki thirteen years to release it. I am reminded of the *Mona Lisa*, and how da Vinci took fifteen years to paint this portrait. In the end, who is it a portrait of? And the quartet, who was it now written for?

Górecki was inspired by Russian poet Velimir Khlebnikov and his poem 'When Horses Die':

When horses die, they sigh,
When grasses die, they shrivel,
When suns die, they flare and expire,
When people die, they sing songs.

And so the quartet was named *Songs Are Sung*, and the songs, hidden and spun out in a trail of cloud in the wind, dissipated through my mind and healed my head.

Górecki was by reputation a fearsome teacher. He would tell his students that if they could live without music for two or three days, then it would be better they spent time with a beer and a woman rather than compose. It does make you wonder what he said to his straight female composition students, but that comment also made me wonder about his life and how music had held on to him, and he on to music, throughout his childhood and beyond.

Górecki's mother died when he was very young, and his stepmother forbade him from playing his mother's piano. His *Symphony of Sorrowful Songs* was a trio of laments for that most sacred of relationships, between parent and child, and here he was composing for the Kronos Quartet, whose first violinist David Harrington was to lose his sixteen-year-old son three years after the quartet was commissioned. The sense of knowing, and acceptance, of Górecki's music drips with every pulse, every strange chord, every note that lies somewhere between embrace and dread.

As the audience, we are the beneficiaries of musicians' dedication to their work. But it goes beyond dedication – it is an obsession, a devotion, an obligation to have this expression of existence come into our world. So many musicians were, and continue to be, impoverished and damaged because of their art. Every day, musicians face fear of financial hardship, fear of not getting a job, fear of losing their job, fear of nobody coming to a concert, fear of many people coming to a concert, fear of a concert being cancelled, fear of breaking a finger, fear of losing a tooth, fear of playing poorly, fear of getting too old, fear of forgetting. There is one thing alone that gives us strength to live a life beyond nightmares: music.

Being transgender is like walking on a tightrope, and I had to hope that the rope would slowly get wider and turn into a path, a road. I knew that if I looked down now, I would fall. I had to keep following my inner compass; I had to keep my head up.

I had written this in *Danger Music* just after my first shot of testosterone, and now I have walked the tightrope for five years. But still, living in your chosen gender, like playing the horn, can be a narrow and perilous path. No matter how sure you are of transitioning, there's a tiny doubt that the hormones won't work, they won't change anything, you'll end up feeling and looking like you always did, you'll have the same problems with a different name.

The tightrope did get wider, but it would also turn narrower, with no warning.

One of the joys and challenges of taking testosterone is that you go into a rapid-onset male puberty. And for me, being in my early fifties, that also meant a rapid-onset menopause. I can hear you going 'ooh, bad' from all sides. The accelerated male puberty meant I suddenly had a ballistic missile of energy, with no experience of how to deal with it. I would go for rides on my motorbike, trying to outrun it. I would go to the gym, trying to outlift it. I would eat the entire contents of the fridge, trying to outweigh it. Nothing worked. I had inexhaustible energy, appetite and frustration. I look on teenage boys now and I feel their pain.

But on top of my hormonal kerfuffle, I was also experiencing menopause. Although I had had a hysterectomy because of fibroids in my late thirties, I still had my ovaries (affectionately called 'the girls'), and with testosterone invading their neighbourhood, the girls were not happy. They had made themselves placards and they were marching up and down inside my abdomen, shouting, 'What about us?' When the testosterone was taking a back seat, the oestrogen would ramp up and tie me down. There were days when I was so suffocated that I could hardly talk.

You can imagine that this duality of energies could not go on. I felt frozen in mind and body, none of it my own. I returned to Dr Bearman, defeated. If this was transition, I had failed. Dr Bearman sent me for blood tests and I returned a few days later.

'Well, Ed, no wonder you're feeling confused. Your testosterone is as high as a young man's, and your oestrogen is as high as thirty-year-old woman's. Your ovaries are, shall we say, Darwinianly robust.'

Great. The one bit of my body I didn't want to work anymore and the girls had decided to go into overtime, with overdrive to boot. I could feel them stamping their boots against my lower abdomen, toasting themselves and their genetic superiority.

'The only thing you can do is wait.'

Waiting, waiting. Practice, practice. Peter Luff, my horn teacher, tells me a cautionary tale of trying to progress too quickly with the wrong technique.

When he was still at music college, Peter had a masterclass with a player from abroad. Sometimes it takes someone from outside to see things clearly. The teacher told Peter that if he didn't change it soon, his embouchure would not last beyond his twenties. Being a young man, Peter shrugged off the comment and headed into his career, playing with the Queensland Symphony Orchestra.

And then, disaster.

The embouchure is created by using muscles throughout your face, going all the way back to your ears. If you put strain on the wrong muscles, and there is insufficient balance and sharing of the workload, the embouchure can simply give up. And that is what happened, spectacularly. One day Peter could play the full range of the horn, the next day he couldn't play a single note.

Peter had a young family. He had been training for this career since he was twelve. What do you do if your face stops working?

You go back to the very beginning, and that is what Peter did. He relearnt how to form and use his embouchure, returning to the simplest of exercises. Going back to the ground floor of elevators, and not even rising an octave. To give an idea of how fundamental this change was, think of something you do every day, something almost beyond thought – driving, or walking, or talking. And now try changing the way you do it. Completely. It seems impossible to enter your mind and body so deeply.

Peter persisted. He combined holiday leave with some careful orchestral rostering and fixed himself. He was back playing after three months, but it took a year or more of remedial work before he could feel secure and healthy again with his playing. It's not surprising to hear that, during this period, he nearly gave up. What a tragedy that would have been. Now he is known internationally as an embouchure doctor, with players from around the world coming to him for help.

We never know what trials the musicians who play for us are going through, which part of their body is starting to fail, what emotions they are having to block to get through a concert, or how much they have had to sacrifice to reach this exalted level. It is simple: if you want to continue to develop on your instrument and maintain a healthy relationship with it, you cannot miss a single day of practice.

'The discipline of practice every day is essential. When I skip a day, I notice a difference in my playing. After two days, the critics notice, and after three days, so does the audience.' (Jascha Heifetz)

'You don't have to practise every day; only on the days you eat.' (Dr Suzuki)

'Have you done your practice today?' (Belinda Manwaring)

Belinda, I'm just about to.

I have been going along to Bardon Strings all year, every Wednesday religiously at 6.30 p.m. Well, sometimes I'm a bit late, but religions are generally forgiving of a lot of things, so wouldn't tardiness be one of them? Anyway, over the months I've gradually got to know a few of the players in the band. To be completely honest, this orchestra deserves a book of its own, but there is one violinist who I wanted to include here because he is so resilient, and so inspiring. His name is Jim.

Jim was born in 1942, the only child of an army serviceman and a homemaker in Atherton, north Queensland. At the age of one, Jim contracted poliomyelitis, a virus that has now been mostly eliminated globally but has killed or paralysed hundreds of thousands of people. There are said to be over four hundred thousand survivors of the disease in Australia alone. But it wasn't until Jim was sixty-four years old that he talked to a doctor about it. When Jim was a child, you just got on with stuff.

Jim's dad became a bank manager after the war, and the family would be moved every few years to, in Jim's words, 'keep the bank johnnies honest'. Jim's mother wanted him to learn music, but music teachers were not exactly around every corner in far north Queensland in the forties and fifties. If there was a teacher, often a nun, she would be a piano teacher, but moving a piano every few years and keeping it in good condition in the humidity was too hard. Instead, Jim was handed a highly portable, highly prized and highly admired instrument: the button accordion. Jim picked up a little knowledge of it here and there and went to dances on the Atherton Tableland where the sole musician would be a button accordionist. By the time he was sent to boarding school in the mid-fifties, Jim saw the accordion as 'his' instrument and could play bush ballads and the popular tunes of the day.

Jim says St Joseph's Nudgee College was the making of him. The Brisbane Catholic school had a strong emphasis on sport, so much so that the rugby teams went from a first fifteen all the way down to a twelfth fifteen. Jim, impressively, was in the seventh fifteen; no allowance was made for Jim's limp but no comment was made on it either. All the boys supported each other, the firsts always cheering on the lowest of the teams. Jim and his friends from Nudgee still meet up several times a year, and have been doing so for the last sixty-one years.

Jim attributes much of his attitude to life to his parents, especially his mother. She was open-hearted, firm and pragmatic with his upbringing, while making sure he had the same opportunities as other children. This allowed Jim to develop a streak of stubbornness: 'I will persist.' Nothing was going to deter him from anything. He went on to university and became a maths and science teacher, but all the while he kept his button accordion with him. In 1968 he was appointed the science and maths teacher at Proston Secondary School, inland from the Sunshine Coast.

'Modern teachers wouldn't believe this but to be able to offer the subjects, we combined the classes. I had twenty Year 8 maths students on my right and twenty-one Year 10 science students on my left, and I taught them all together. That was interesting. Young teachers didn't get much sympathy from me when they complained about class sizes.'

Jim was also delegated to be the music teacher at Proston; his qualifications were he could play the button accordion and he liked to sing. Those were the days. He eventually went to work in Townsville and lived at a residential college run by the Franciscan order. It was here that Jim heard classical violinist Jan Sedivka, the legendary professor from Tasmania, accompanied by Larry Sitsky, perform a Beethoven sonata for the Townsville Chamber Music Society. Jim was transfixed. This was his introduction to classical music and in the same year, 1970, Jim heard a live orchestra for the first time when the Queensland Symphony Orchestra went on a regional tour.

In 1973 Jim's three-year self-funded trip to study history, politics and government at the University of Kent, Canterbury, England, meant he took a break from the button accordion. At London's Covent Garden, Jim had the chance to experience opera for the first time, just like Charlie. When he returned to Australia he had no money left, so he returned to his parents' house in Brisbane, where he still lives. It is a sturdy, modest brick bungalow on one of the languorous terraces of northwest Brisbane, overlooking the distant city. Jim took a position at Kedron State High School and remained there for thirty-two years. One of the teachers, Bob McLaren, was a bush musician and decided in 1982 there should be a school bush band. Jim joined the band and moved from a two-row to a three-row accordion, and played classics like *Click Go the Shears*, *Botany Bay* and *Moreton Bay*. Eventually, a string-playing teacher came to the school, and Jim started to teach himself the mandolin. When Jim was forty-nine, he decided he would like to have a go on the violin. As he says, he is a great one for aspirations, so he went along to the music shop and bought himself a good French violin, which he still plays today.

The challenges for Jim in going from accordion and mandolin to the violin were mostly with the bow. But Jim found a patient teacher, Tim Butcher.

'I rang up Tim, and started in 1993. Talk about persistence, from him and me. Probably coming through the effects of polio – persistence, persistence. You just break it down and keep on going. I went to him once a week for twenty-something years. His method was very good: scales, arpeggios, then some fiddle tunes, then classical tunes. Tim would say, "You're getting close!" and we'd go on to another one. Then in 2017, Tim said he'd heard there was a new orchestra starting.'

That orchestra was Bardon Strings.

Jim is sitting in the first violin section right now, playing *Gypsy Airs* by Sarasate. His beloved French violin under his chin, Jim looks at his music and to the conductor, Anne, with his bright, dark eyes. His hair is neatly parted, just turning a little grey at seventy-six. Jim is wiry, with the body of the runner he would like to be but his limp is now more pronounced, the late effects of polio taking their toll. But they don't affect his violin playing. When Anne stops and asks the first violins to play on their own you can hear Jim's sound, free and clear. He is a boy again, playing for a dance.

From all those years ago when Jim's parents wanted him to play music, they would have been delighted to see what music has given him. Jim still plays in a bush band and comes to Bardon Strings every week. In his life so far, Jim has experienced many things we can all share, and they are tied together with music.

'Music has made me much more sociable. And the good thing about it is, everyone wants you to play well. It's not about competitiveness, like competing in sport. Music depends on everyone playing as well as they can. Music is for the people.'

———————————————

I am in a lesson with Megan, one of my adult cello students. Megan is in her early fifties and started playing the cello three years ago, completely from scratch. From knowing zero about music, apart from having wonderfully eclectic taste in listening, Megan now reads music, is learning music theory and harmony, plays Beethoven and Dvořák and Bach with a full, rich sound and vibrato, and has performed in several solo and group concerts. Megan is proof that you can learn music as an adult, and that you will learn as much and as well as a child. A while ago, Megan was learning part of a viola da gamba sonata by J.S. Bach, transcribed for cello. The music is highly contrapuntal, weaving different strands around in a maze of rhythm, like a conga line that has split in two to double the dance. Finn, a teenage student, once commented that this music didn't really have a tune, but then he found himself whistling it after his lesson. 'Oh, it does have a tune!'

Megan has her own adult version of the music's character. 'It sounds like a drunk dude at a bar, rambling on and changing subjects every sentence.'

The piece is perky and jaunty and skips through the dancefloor. There are a few tricky bits; Megan worked on these by isolating them, practising the string crossings by taking away the left hand, then practising the left hand by taking away the complex bowing. There is a small part in the middle of the music where all the difficulty falls away and you are left with two long notes. Whole notes.

Music rhythm is simple division. The words for different lengths of notes sound arcane – breve, semibreve, minim, crochet, quaver, semiquaver, demisemiquaver and hemidemisemiquaver (I'm not kidding). Americans take the arcaneness away and call the notes by their divisions, starting from a semibreve (a breve is very rarely used). Therefore, a semibreve is a whole note, then a minim is a half note, a crochet is a quarter note, and so on, all the way to a sixty-fourth note. This certainly makes teaching rhythm easier, but I also enjoy the moment when I can teach the other names. They bring the poetry back.

When we reach the whole notes, the semibreves, in the Bach, instead of them being an easy spot to regroup and relax, they can seem difficult. We have become used to intricacy, and we don't want to believe this moment can be this simple. We have become so used to one way of being that when we are presented with an elementary option, we blindly crash through it. We get lost in the simple parts because we are focused on the distant challenge.

Megan plays the semibreve, and I can see she is counting – one, two, three, four. And the next one – one, two, three, four. And then we are back. To the busyness of life. To the running and the counterpoint.

Megan smiles. She has done it. She has been resilient enough to practise the hard bits, but she has also learnt when she can let go of resilience, to enjoy the simple moment.

Megan has made her notes whole.

D:
KINDNESS

Music doesn't get in. Music is already in. Music simply uncovers what is there.

MATT HAIG, *HOW TO STOP TIME*

KINDNESS IS AT THE HEART of all religious teaching, and it is at the heart of music.

As we go through our lives, sediment builds up – in our body, our mind and our nature. We live with hatred and love, both of ourselves and others, and sometimes in equal measure. Just as Mrs Izod declared we are born knowing everything and slowly forget it, the sediment builds up and up, covering our senses and our sense until we don't know anything anymore. To recover ourselves, to clear ourselves, there must be a catharsis of our whole. We try different ways – more exercise, more knowledge, more travel, more food, more friends, more sleep, more work – but it is all simply a distraction from the real work, which is to look inside. Other art forms can bring us to the precipice – visual art, dance, literature – but to access the absolute, we must go beyond words and logic and physical form to the heart of the universe itself: sound.

Some types of music are better suited to this process than others.

If you spend most of your listening time with Western music, you will be used to hearing a melody developed with harmony. Whether it's Joni Mitchell and her otherworldly tinge of heaven around her song or Rachmaninoff and his occasional jazz chords, Western music is built on a progressive vertical structure. Listen to Bach and his harmonies support a cathedral. Listen to Radiohead and their harmonies hold you up in your sadness. Indian classical music is the opposite, as it does not have the same harmonic underpinning; it has a home note, but the melody does not develop with harmony – it develops with momentum, rhythm, repetition and concentration. Some Indian ragas have only five notes, yet they can be played for hours, and at the end you feel you have travelled the galaxy. Because there is no distracting change in what is underneath the notes, we are forced to listen to the notes themselves. They become the unwavering gaze of a great teacher: we cannot look away, we can only submit. We fill our lives with distraction so we do not have to listen to what is inside our heads, but music gives us the coherence to finally clear ourselves. Music is our lighthouse.

Your child is six years old. They have leukaemia, so they need to be tested regularly. Every two weeks they are taken into a hospital theatre and doctors perform a lumbar puncture, which involves inserting a hollow needle between two vertebrae and withdrawing cerebrospinal fluid. Your child is given a small amount of sedative, but it isn't usually enough.

And there is something unusual about the room they are in: it is soundproofed so the children outside cannot hear the screams from the children inside.

This was the method for spinal taps when Dr Catherine Crock began her work as a doctor in Melbourne in the 1990s. Dr Crock had come from a family world filled with music, but she stepped into a clinical world filled with sterility. Dr Crock knew there was something missing in the hospital, that something needed to change, so she sat down with the children's families and asked them how they thought the environment could be improved. The families suggested putting the children to sleep for painful or traumatic procedures and using music to help calm them, so Dr Crock started to play recordings of Mozart and Beethoven in the theatre and waiting area. But it didn't always help. She realised that intense orchestral music, like the final movements of Beethoven symphonies, were making the children more anxious.

This was only twenty years ago, but it's still hard to imagine how sidelined music was in the hospital. In the 1990s there was only one part-time music therapist for the whole hospital, as music therapy still hadn't been recognised as 'core business', as it is now. Dr Crock knew she needed scientific evidence for anything to change institutionally, so she presented data to hospital administrations around the country that proved how, in the long term, doing painful things to heal children was damaging. The children didn't forget the trauma of their treatment, which meant they developed a phobia of hospitals and medicine and would try to avoid going to the doctor when they needed to go. Administrations started to look at pain management in a broader sense, and Dr Crock founded a system called Comfort Kids, where the child was first given play and music therapy and then, after this comfort, was put to sleep for their procedure.

Dr Crock describes the sounds of a hospital, in a normal setting.

'There are mechanical sounds of trolleys going by, metal on metal, instruments on a tray, lots of beeping of monitors – blood pressure, pulse rate, oxygen saturation. When they are too low or too high, or if a drip is running out, they will start to beep. Those sounds are very jarring, and they need to be so they can alert staff to something going wrong. And there's background chatter, staff calling out to each other, all necessary, but it can be disturbing. Sound levels in hospitals are as disturbing as the fluorescent lighting. Even more so. Sound goes straight into the middle of the brain.'

To control the type of music played in the hospital setting, Dr Crock went on to create a collection of specially composed and recorded music for children's hospitals called *Hush*. There are eighteen albums now, and the contributing musicians are a who's who of the Australian classical world. Best of all, their music is played in hospitals all around the country. As Dr Crock says, now the mood in the waiting rooms is one of joy and fun, and the families' focus is not on the procedure ahead but on being part of that joy.

These revolutionary ideas continue to help not only the patients and their families but also the composers who create the music.

Matthew Hindson is an Australian composer and professor of composition at the Sydney Conservatorium of Music. Matthew has been composing for decades, so you might think being asked to compose a piece for the thirteenth album of Hush music was simply another, albeit important, post along the way. But Dr Crock ensures that this is not the case for her musicians. As part of the process, Dr Crock brings the composers to the Royal Children's Hospital in Melbourne to see and hear and feel what the patients and families are experiencing. Matthew attended a child's lumbar puncture, and, as he says, it was the start of a musical epiphany for him: the realisation that music is not something to be created merely for self-expression but that it can be used in service for a higher good, for transcendence, if just in that moment.

Matthew finished a composition for the project called *Sophie's Song*, but on the due date he listened to it again and realised he needed to give something more of himself, something kinder. And he did.

The Stars Above Us All begins with such fulsome hope that you are compelled to lift your eyes upwards. The sound is a dream of safety with each note from the celeste, the friendliest of instruments, marking a new star in the firmament above. Hindson creates the music for that indefinable moment, a lingering between consciousness and sleep, that moment when we float unanchored in our mind. And his music has not been the same since this work. As he says, 'I have a whole new reason to write; it's opened up a new side of what I want to do. I've always asked, why am I writing music when all these other composers have done such amazing things? It's because I can respond to the situations I'm in now, as an Australian composer: whether it's responding to an adolescent going through a mental health issue, or just wanting to contribute to that sense of transcendence people might feel, getting really lost in music. Hush has given me permission to do that.'

Music, the right kind of music, calms and gives hope and optimism to the clinical staff as well.

Dr Crock explains.

'It's something we weren't really aiming at, thinking how it affects the staff working in an environment like this every day. I think Covid has made that even more obvious, the stress health professionals are under in their everyday jobs. And the sound environment is a big part of that. We're working in a chaotic cacophony of noise for eight to ten hours at a time, with alarms you have to respond to and beeps you know mean something.'

Dr Crock describes an emergency in the theatre.

'A four-year-old boy was being given an anaesthetic and was just about to go off to sleep. That's a critical time, when something can go wrong: they can stop breathing or have a spasm in their throat, they maybe swallow the wrong way or they're disturbed. It can make everyone really tense and people can snap at each other. But this particular time, the team handled the emergency beautifully and smoothly. And in the debrief, the nursing staff said, "The music playing in the background made such a difference – it kept the mood as calm as possible, so we could respond better as a team."'

Every day at work, Dr Crock has a team huddle to start the day. She goes into the room first to put on some music, and then the team talks through the theatre list and how they will interact with each other, how they will function, the potential stress points, and the importance of being kind to each other.

You can't impose kindness, but you can induce it. Music induces kindness.

From a time when little children were being treated in soundproof rooms, a nightmare that provoked lifelong phobias of medical care, Dr Crock's team has transformed the culture of treatment in children's hospitals. She tells the story of a little boy, five years old.

'The boy's family were recently from Vietnam and we had to use an interpreter to explain all the things that would be happening as he went through his cancer treatment. He would have to come every week for the first four weeks to have a lumbar puncture and bone marrow tests, then, on the fifth week, he wouldn't need to come for a month.'

On the fifth week Dr Crock went to the waiting area and the family were sitting out there.

'Oh no, I thought, we didn't explain this properly to them! So we called down the interpreter again and explained to the parents that they didn't need to be there. And the dad said, "Yes, we know. Thanh just came to hear the music."'

_____

The music carries you in your cot, swaying on the deepest water. The piano begins, a kind pulse, note on note, each chord holding gentle hands with the next, and the violin dreaming above. The chords walk in a wide circle, a spiralling upwards, and the source is touched again and the violin quickens, ever higher, until the original octave is a speck, far, far below. As the music soars it elevates you until you are flying, like Icarus, up into the sun.

Mercy by Max Richter.

How can you be unchanged after hearing this music? How can your very cells not be softened in the marinade of its sound? We can look cerebrally at Richter's music and analyse it – a passacaglia, three beats in a bar over a repeated bass line – or we can understand the music at a deeper level, the level of our senses. We can listen and we can feel the music sinking into us, and ourselves sinking into the music to release emotion we may not have felt in a long time, perhaps ever. We listen and we accept our own complexities and their endlessness, and the kindness and mercy within us all.

———————————

I wish I could say my horn playing is elevating you ever higher. I wish I could say my horn playing is carrying you in a cot, swaying on the deepest water. What I can say is that my horn playing is like the early days of human flight: inventive, admirable but seriously unsafe. I am a horn-playing Icarus, constantly falling from the sky. My playing is earthward-bound, and I'm still standing on the original octave.

I am, in a word, stuck.

I know I'm not really stuck, only in my ego-driven mind. Still, when you try for high(ish) notes and you fall off them time after time, like bullets ricocheting off a wall, it's a challenge to believe you are making any progress.

'Remember the process. Follow the process, and you are bound to be successful.'

Peter Luff's words echo through my head and every day I follow the process, trusting him implicitly. I play my elevators especially for my remaining neighbours (the other neighbours left; they demolished the house next door – I'm actually not kidding) and I walk on, walk on with Anton Horner and his studies. Dear Anton. It feels like we've moved in together.

Some days it really doesn't sound too shabby. I play a G just above the stave and the sound is perhaps not golden and heroic but at least not the emergency red it once was. Then the next day I do exactly the same thing – same breath, same embouchure, same thought – and the G is like a child in Victorian times, seen but not heard. Argh! My ego says thank you to Peter for telling me students don't generally progress this far this fast, but it is also a dangerous thing to say to a Type-A personality. Now I just want to go further. Will I never learn? I am obsessed with high notes like the mountaineer George Mallory was with Everest. And look what happened to him.

The horn has the reputation of being one of the hardest instruments for a very good reason. A millimetre of movement in your embouchure, a slight lack of support from your diaphragm, a different colour shirt on your horn-blowing body that day and you miss the note. Did I say argh?

I admit it. I love how hard it is. I love how much I need to think, concentrate, assimilate and work my body. I love how much I am learning about my lungs, mind and spirit. I love that there is no fast track to improving. I love that there is no good, no bad, just process or no process. All I can do is – you've got it – follow the process.

To distract myself I decide to get to know my horn in another way, by cleaning her. Anna does not have any lacquer and she looks a little bit patchy, like Winston, the tabby cat I had when I was a kid. Winston was a lovely cat who licked himself a lot to keep clean. I know horns are amazing but not self-licking, so I call the local horn shop, Brass Music Specialists, and ask them how to clean my pride and joy.

I receive a surprising answer.

I am used to the highly specialised world of string playing where, if you want to clean your string instrument, you need to buy a microscopic bottle of a creamy alchemic something that costs all your whisky money for the month and can only be applied under the new moon with a cloth woven from baby squirrels' tails.

So you can imagine my surprise when the dude at the brass shop tells me to go down to Supercheap Auto and buy some Autosol metal polish, and that an old t-shirt will do to wipe it off.

I tap the phone in my hand, making sure the speaker doesn't have an insect in it.

'I'm sorry, can I just check, did you say Supercheap Auto?' Imagine that in a snotty English accent. Sorry, brass dude.

'Yes, that's it. Get the big tube. It's even cheaper.'

I invite Charlie and Happy on a drive and we go down to the local shopping centre where there is, da-dah, a Supercheap Auto. I want to ask the assistant to direct me to the horn aisle but decide it probably isn't in my best interests. I find the tube and, yes, I buy a big one, and pick up a cover for my motorbike at the same time.

Oh gosh, why didn't I take up the horn when I was younger? Motorbike and horn shopping simultaneously. So satisfying. You don't get that with the viola.

———————————

'Wait! WAIT! Listen! Watch!'

I can still feel those words, let alone hear them, being yelled at the viola section, no, every section, in orchestra rehearsals at the Royal Northern College of Music thirty years ago. Huh, I'm kidding myself – *thirty-five* years ago. The conductor, Timothy Reynish, was sounding and looking personally upset that we hadn't waited for whichever instrument had the melody at that moment. If you are playing the accompaniment, which viola players always do (apart from those three bars in Shostakovich's fifth symphony), you must wait for the melody to move, you must listen for the changes in harmony, you must watch for the conductor to give the subtlest of signals, and then you must wait again. There is no barging through when you play music with others. An orchestra is a benign dictatorship, where the conductor expects obedience, discipline and camaraderie from their citizens. Music students around the world, especially orchestral instrumentalists, will have had these words yelled at them countless times in orchestral rehearsals, and for good reason – music students are our future, and they cannot be allowed to fail. Just think of the consequences. The orchestra rehearsal is as important as personal practice.

The etymology of the word rehearsal is surprising; I had always thought it came from re-hearing something, but it's more profound than that. 'Re' is again, but the middle syllable, 'hears', comes from the Old French *hercier*, to rake or harrow, which itself comes the Old French word for plough or harrow, *herce*. A harrow, in case you haven't used one recently, is a tool for breaking up clods of earth, raking over the soil, pulling up weeds and covering the new seed.

So when we rehearse, we are digging up and turning over our music, pulling out the weeds of poor phrasing or intonation or ensemble, and preparing the soil of the sound to create a perfect place for sowing seed. When we rehearse, we are bringing our combined energy and imagination to one point. In the best rehearsal, we are sowing seeds for the growth of a deep-rooted performance, a performance that will stand the test of time.

When we go to a professional orchestral concert, we expect the orchestra to have the timing of a Swiss watch, the emotions of a Shakespeare play, the agility of a ballet dancer, the ease of a Broadway actor, the balance of a Hollywood sound engineer and the soul of a mystic. We expect technical and musical perfection as their audience, but not as much as the players expect technical and musical perfection from themselves and each other. Musicians spend years, six or more, at music college, developing the skills to be able to perform the most complex of music under enormous pressure, and it is only through the kindness of our teachers exhorting us to do better that we get anywhere at all.

One hundred people playing together in a full symphony orchestra is a superlative achievement, and it can only be achieved by proper rehearsal, the technique of which must be learnt. When a music student learns the art of rehearsing, they become a link in the chain of kindness, in turn passing on that kindness to the students of the future.

For all the thousands of times Tim Reynish yelled at me and my fellow students, I say thank you a million times. And although I choose not to yell, I do my best to pass on that wisdom as fully as I can.

Wait. Listen. Watch.

And the instrument Tim Reynish played before he became a conductor? The horn.

———————————

There's a joke about viola players – actually, there are hundreds of jokes about viola players, but my favourite is this one.

A conductor of an orchestra decided she would do some team building by encouraging the different sections of the orchestra to go out hunting snails. Perhaps it was a French conductor. Anyway, the first section to fill a bucket got to choose the music in their next concert. The trumpet section came first, with their snails a bit trampled and mixed in with some beer cans, the cello section next, with their snails all neatly put on skewers, then the flute section, with their snails wrapped in clarinet music. After a while, all the sections of the orchestra had filled their snail buckets. All except one: the violas. The conductor went deep into the paddock to look for them and there they were, the whole section huddled around an empty bucket, looking forlorn.

'Hey, how come you haven't caught even one snail?' the conductor asked, looking incredulous.

The principal viola stood up, defeated.

'Well, we would sneak up on a snail, then ... whoosh! It was gone!'

As a viola player for, hang on a minute, oh yes, forty-two years, I have delighted in the special vibe of the viola. Sure, we can play as fast as the violins, but why would you want to? The art of the viola player is to sit inside the music: we are the engine in the car, the chocolate in the croissant, the muscle in the body. Without the violas, music has no substance.

Viola parts in orchestral pieces often involve counting very, very long notes, and very, very long rests. We are the chill people of the orchestra, along with the double bassists. But as young musicians (even viola players) learn to play more and more notes and to use their instruments in more and more sophisticated ways, there comes a watershed moment when the feeling is so pleasurable that they simply do not want to stop playing. And for music teachers this moment is glorious, but it can also be dangerous.

Music is made up of sounds and silence – the notes and the rests in between, which give the notes resonance and significance. Without rests in music there would be no punctuation or reflection. Rests provide a veil of safety and light to perceive the world. Like empty space in photographs or paintings, rests show the importance of what is there by acknowledging what is not there.

Many years ago in Hong Kong, I had a young viola student; let's call her Julie. When she played the viola, her aim was to play everything as fast and as loud as possible, with not a care for the sound or the grace of the music. Julie's mother had a very high-profile job in something businessy and would brusquely nod at me the few times I saw her. Julie was an only child and when she wasn't doing one of her many extra activities, she seemed to spend most of her time with her nanny, who looked perpetually tormented. Julie's playing reflected the situation of her family life: unloved and desperate. Through her music, Julie seemed to be expressing a desire to grab attention – somebody's, anybody's, even if it was just a boring old viola teacher who kept asking you to slow down. I beseeched Julie in every way I could think to take more care with the music, to show it some kindness, but she just shrugged her shoulders and said, 'Whatever.'

To be kind to others, we need to be kind to ourselves. To be kind to ourselves, we need time for reflection, for rest, for consideration and determination. Julie was being rushed through her life from one activity to the next, and the viola was just another thing to get through before she could go to sleep and forget her existence. Music can guide us to inner silence, but in Julie's life it had guided her to inner cacophony.

Julie gave up the viola when she was ten.

If I had to wager, I would bet my life that Rosie will never give up the cello. When she plays, her eyes gaze into the absent present and she lives beyond herself, yet completely inside herself. Rosie is grace in music.

We have come to the middle of the year, so it's time to have a concert. Some students hate performing and I need to bring them very gently to the performance space, but Rosie only needs a little persuasion. Since Covid is still trailing its tentacles, we need to limit the audience to a select group: her family and her teddy bears. I use the term 'teddy bear' loosely, as the group includes the world's largest pink unicorn and what looks like a giant snail, but then I wonder, who would have a snail as a toy? Still, the good thing about toys with fixed eyes is that they are always, always paying attention. No coughing, no rustling of lolly wrappers, just settled and waiting and listening. Admittedly, their applause is a little quiet, but the human beings, as opposed to the stuffed beings, can make up for them in that regard.

I, as the teacher, am the back-up band. I encourage Rosie to introduce the music in her clearest reading-out-loud voice –

no mumbling! smile, make the audience feel comfortable, thank them for coming and bow deeply at the applause. And say 'hippopotamus' at the bottom of the bow for perfect bow timing.

The audience stares back a little blankly as Rosie introduces each piece: *Back to Baroque; Long, Long Ago; Twinkle, Twinkle;* and, a personal favourite, *Stew Pot Hop.* Rosie settles herself before each piece, makes sure her feet are firmly on the ground and her bow hold is soft, her left hand settled and rounded, and her core strong and engaged. She sings the first few notes in her head to make sure she's going in the right direction then she's off, as committed as an arrow to its target. Some people naturally hold an audience's attention and Rosie is one of them. And look, I don't want to speak for the unicorn, but I think the teddy bears were really into it.

After the concert, as the audience is taken away back to their beds and shelves, there's a slight tinge left of the music – the carefully positioned chair, the music stand still up, and a feeling from Rosie that now, after her first ever concert, now she is really a musician.

What is the kindness of music? How can music, by listening or playing it, induce kindness in ourselves? One of the ways I feel music allows me to be kinder is by showing me the simple perfection of the here and now. Music is unholdable, therefore the only way to experience it is by letting go. Music, exquisite music, brings you to the eternal present and disintegrates any desire to move beyond that moment. And when the music ends you are left suspended, transcendent.

If you can, listen to a single piece of music called *In Paradisum*, by the Ukraine-born Estonian composer Galina Grigorjeva. It's short, just four minutes, so about as long as your average pop song. Grigorjeva composed the music in 2012 for an a cappella choir.

The music floats out of nothing – it has always been there and it always will be. The high voices hang in the air, waiting, watching, until lower voices come to bring their foundations to earth. The music stretches into the past and future, hanging, a suspension bridge in the mist, flickering in and out of sight and never complete, the line of singers moving forward, individually yet together, across the harbour. And then, on the final fathomless chord, we reach the other side.

The setting of *In Paradisum* is sometimes used in Christian funeral services as the body is taken out of the church, and the Latin text speaks of angels taking us to heaven and leading us to eternal life. But I believe this music alone can take us to our own eternal life, here on earth, by identifying and eliciting the kernel of our true selves – kindness.

———————————————

I have been moving around for most of my life. When I last bothered to work it out, I have lived in over forty different houses in a few different countries. When people asked why I was always moving, I would explain that it was my nature, that I was happiest being a slight outsider to life. I told myself it was easier to observe as an outsider but failed to tell myself that it's easier to lie to yourself as an outsider. If you're always on the move, you never need to face who you really are. It took moving to Brisbane, and starting my transition, to accept myself wholly.

In Brisbane I landed on a cushion of good fortune. Moving to this city was the best thing I have done in my life. There were the hiccups of finding a job, but Charlie and her family and friends pulled me into their sphere and held me tightly in a loving embrace. Musically, I also landed on the fortune cushion when I started learning how to teach the Suzuki cello method from the cellist Belinda Manwaring on the Gold Coast. I had wanted to play the cello when I was eight because I heard a recording of Jacqueline du Pré, so it seemed like the completion of a circle when I found out Belinda had had a lesson with Jacqueline in London in the early 1980s. She was a superstar to Belinda as well.

'My earliest memory of Jacqueline was when my grandmother took me to see her play in the Sydney Town Hall when I was nine. It's one of my memories that is etched in my brain. We had an aisle seat and she played Elgar with Daniel Barenboim. It must have been 1969, a couple of years before she got sick. I remember she lost the hairs off her bow and she was ripping them off – very flamboyant, in a beautiful red dress. She was my absolute idol.'

In 1980, during her last year at the Sydney Conservatorium, Belinda went to England and arranged to have a lesson with her musical heroine. Belinda called du Pré's secretary and the following Tuesday took the tube from Kilburn to Knightsbridge and stood in front of Jacqueline du Pré's garden gate, cello by her side. She was buzzed in, ushered to the hallway and there, on the left, was the music room – a grand piano and two cello cases underneath it, probably containing her Davidoff Stradivarius and her preferred cello, a Peresson. At this point in her illness, Jacqueline was far too sick to ever play them again. Belinda began to warm up, and the nurse brought in Jacqueline in her wheelchair.

'It was one of the most shocking things in my life – she looked nothing like I remembered her. She was this old-looking lady, all her red hair was gone, she was *very* hard to understand, but she was very nice. Very calm. I tried to book another lesson a few weeks later, but the secretary said her health had deteriorated. So I only had that one lesson, but it was something I will never forget.'

Jacqueline du Pré's legacy was a whole generation of cellists, who begat their own generation of cellists, and Belinda is contributing her own part by playing and teaching in southeast Queensland and instructing cellists in how to teach the Suzuki method. I had learnt a little about it when I was teaching in

Kabul, a method of learning based around music being a language: if you can learn your mother tongue, you can learn music through the same process of exposure and repetition. Anyone can set themselves up as a music teacher, but to be a Suzuki teacher you need to take an audition, attend group training sessions and lessons, and have your own students and teaching assessed by your teacher trainer, in my case, Belinda. You learn how each piece, right from the start with *Twinkle* to the very end with a virtuosic Boccherini concerto, is interconnected. One leads to the next in a technically and musically logical way.

The love parents bestow on their children is often assumed; they are their offspring, after all. But when you think of the love and kindness teachers bestow on their students, it is a unique demonstration of unconditional love – love for the education and development of the student in the broadest sense, but also unconditional love for the art form itself, for music.

Nowadays, music teachers work under conditions that may have been unimaginable just a few years ago: reduced funding, reduced time, reduced facilities and equipment, and, perhaps most importantly, reduced respect for the value of what they do.

Music teachers are part of a noble line stretching back to Bach and beyond. Many of our teachers can personally trace their musical heritage back to Beethoven, to Mozart, Clara Schumann, Peter Sculthorpe. There is an unbroken song of music that our teachers hold gently in their callused fingers and hearts, because they know they are the keepers of this knowledge for our generation. They have the great privilege of passing it on to the next generation, and the duty of passing it on in better condition than when they received it.

Being a musician, but particularly also teaching music, is more important than ever in our computer age. Some of our young folk are influenced by a negative screen culture, spending hours and hours and hours playing video games, on social media, and losing a sense of their self-worth within a dysfunctional field of criticism and conformity. The importance of 'I', not just in the names of products but in the strong egotistical culture of our time, means that music is, even more, a saviour; it is one of the main activities, along with team sports, where our young people can experience the value of putting yourself last.

Music teachers not only lift our young people from the labyrinth of social media but they also lift them to a place inaccessible any other way: they provide a gateway to a part of the universe that cannot be described in words, or in painting, or in movement, only in sound.

Being a musician is important, but being a music teacher is more important. They give succour when our lives are wrecked. They give momentum when we need to celebrate. They give inner peace when all around is turmoil. They soak their students' lives in music. They are the doctors of our spirits, and they always will be, whether their students become professional musicians or not. Because they never stop being a musician, and they never stop teaching; they know it is a great privilege, a great responsibility, and it is the greatest joy of all.

Belinda showed her kindness to me not by letting me get away with poor sound or sloppy rhythm but the opposite: by being as exacting as she could be, and by showing her own dedication with her glorious playing. Every few weeks I have a lesson with Belinda and she hears my slightly sorry rendition of Bach, or Lully, or Haydn, and she waits patiently, all the time considering and observing and calculating what, in this lesson, will be the best thing for her to talk about, what will be the observations that will carry me forward the furthest to the next lesson. Will it be my bow arm, or my phrasing, or my shifting, or my sound? Will it be something very specific, or will it be a general comment that includes all those points with one sweep? As Belinda says, she focuses on the bow hand because that's much more difficult and the left hand tends to sort itself out, although, with me coming from viola, my left hand is as troublesome as my right. Whatever it is, Belinda always gives the perfect amount of help, with clear practical advice about how to make my playing better.

'The bulk of my teaching is teaching people how to practise. You learn from your own bitter experience: if you're practising for eight hours a day and you still play out of tune in the concert, something has gone wrong. It's not the hours you've put in, it's that the method you've used is faulty. I give my students practical advice; I don't just say, practise more,

I show them how. And I give them clear guidelines for what we are learning, and I give them responsibility for their own development.'

Most teachers are able to tell you what is wrong, but it is only the very best teachers who will hold back much of that advice and mention only the most fruitful for that stage of development. Some teachers teach from ego, some from necessity, some from frustration, some from duty, but the very best teachers teach from tenderness.

When I started to learn the cello in my early thirties, I decided to give up the viola completely, so I could let my body adjust to the new feeling of playing. It took a decade until it felt safe to go back to the viola, finally sure in my cello ability. I had reached a point where my cello playing helped my viola playing, and vice versa. Just as learning an instrument takes persistence, practice and sometimes sheer bloody-mindedness, over the last few years I have been practising how to be around men, as a man. In my previous life, most of my friends were women and I had relationships with women. I grew up in a family dominated by women and went to a girls school. I knew very little about how men talk, interact, how they just *are*.

As I needed to let go of the viola to play the cello, would I have to give up my identity completely to successfully transition? Or was there a middle way?

One thing I noticed immediately was that it was impossible to be chatty with women I didn't know. Once, while waiting to pay for a shirt in a menswear shop, I tried to make conversation with the shop assistant, asking what she was doing over the weekend.

'I'm going to a barbecue *with my husband*,' she snapped, not meeting my eye.

Previously, I would have had a chat with women on planes, buses, the supermarket aisles, but I cannot do that anymore – I always get the vibe of 'you're being slimy; back off'. Which I completely understand. I would have done the same thing. If I'm walking down a street in the evening, I will cross to the other side if I see a woman coming; I know she will cross over if I don't.

And when men speak with men, what do they talk about and how do they say it? One time, very early on in my transition, Charlie and I went to a birthday party. Charlie headed into the kitchen and was having a ball with a group of women, laughing and hugging and crying and generally delighting in that complex warp and weft of conversation women will create. Meanwhile, I was left standing around in a circle of men, all of us with a beer in our hands, all of us silent and eyeing each other up, as if it was an ancient contest for the leadership of the tribe. There was no way I was going to start the conversation, which is something I would have easily done before. I stood quietly, observing, waiting.

Finally, after a rigid silence, a chap opposite nodded to me, gestured with his beer, and asked, 'So, what sort of car do you drive?'

This was the only time I wondered whether I had made a terrible mistake.

Another of the areas I continue to find tricky about transitioning from female to male is taking my top off in public. Fifty years of being told to keep your top on means that now, when I can easily take my top off, I feel vulnerable and, well, naked. My chest surgery has healed so well that you cannot see any scars at all, but I still feel locked in an old way of being, which I want to snap myself out of. I want to be more physically effusive but lack the courage. I take the warning from Dr Bearman very seriously that testosterone is a powerful drug and that I need to respect it by using my body, or my body will betray me.

I've just had my fifty-fourth birthday, so middle age is establishing itself, starting with my middle (is that why it's called middle age?). Over the last couple of months I've felt a need to shake things up a bit, move some dust from my inner shelves, vacuum under the bed (I'm trying to get rid of attachment, but I've still got the vacuum ones), grow some muscles and find something new.

But then I thought, aha, I don't need something new. What I need is something old.

So, like pulling out a leather jacket that you last wore twenty years ago, I have gone back to an old love: the swimming pool.

Although, just like that jacket, the fit has changed over the years. Okay, it doesn't appear to fit at all.

First of all, I am now officially a wimp. It is currently thirty-four degrees Celsius in Brisbane. The water in our local pool is heated. So why, oh why, do I shiver when I lower myself in and think about mulled wine and blankets?

Secondly, I am now an amorphous mass in the water. Where once I was smooth and unsplashy, now I'm a water troll. Other swimmers leave the lane I'm in to avoid the churning vortex of chlorine they might otherwise be drawn into. I've become 'that' swimmer at the pool. I swim at 1 p.m., so you know now when to avoid me.

Something had to be done. I am determined that I *will* fit into this jacket again, even it becomes a strait one. I need help, big time.

This is when you call in the assistance of old friends, especially ones who are excellent swimmers, know about the use of imagery in teaching (particularly for a little ol' viola player like me) and, most important of all, are kind.

Enter pool left Helentherese, my swim coach.

I've known Helentherese since we were in the Hong Kong Philharmonic together in the early nineties, and she was another gift waiting for me in Brisbane. HT has gone on to heights of professional beauty with her violin, is a Churchill Fellow, and is also a smooth and stylish swimmer. HT is basically the person you want beside you in either a music or a swimming crisis.

We meet at a university pool. I feel this is a good start: somehow those university swimmers will leave some swimming knowledge behind. All I find is a twig at the bottom of the pool as I go underwater to try to put on some fins. These, HT promises, will give me some buoyancy as I perfect my stroke.

See? Already things are looking up. The use of the verb 'perfect' anywhere near my level of swimming may be the equivalent to saying to your small child, as you remove their bicycle training wheels, that next year they are bound to win the Tour de France, but I don't mind. I'll take any form of encouragement, even a wacky one.

Fins finally secured, HT takes me through my paces. She is kindness personified. She lets me do a couple of lazy laps with just my legs. Wow, fins are good! Just as I'm wondering how I can get my feet to grow, HT suggests we do some drills with our hands as fists.

What? I thought you were supposed to cup your hands a little bit and keep your fingers together. Huh. Australians. What do they know about swimming?

Ah, I see now that it's an excellent exercise in engaging the full arm and not relying on just the hand.

HT. So smart. I'm feeling pretty pleased with myself for predicting she would be the best swim coach for me. I see the Olympics beckoning.

HT spreads icing on the swimming lesson cake by suggesting I think about my stroke like a bowing arm for my viola. She then invites me for actual cake after the lesson.

As a little bonus, at the end we dip our toes into tumble turns. Although apparently, in grown-up language these are not called tumble turns but racing turns.

Once again, my confidence takes a flying leap. We are swimming in a university pool. I have fins. I can achieve perfection. We are going to do the turny thing that Michael Phelps does. All I need to do is pretend I'm playing my viola. I begin to wonder about actually playing my viola in the pool when HT demonstrates a turn.

Oh gosh. That looks hard. True, I have seen small children do it, but still, this is not just dipping your toe into the water. This is submerging your entire head and breathing apparatus.

I announce to HT that I will only try it if I can hold my nose.

'You cannot. Michael Phelps doesn't hold his nose.'

Good point. And with that I tumble to my fate.

It is not pretty. I should have been wearing more clothes, so they could have had a wash in the torrent.

I stand up at the end, feeling somewhat pleased with myself that I didn't die.

'Hmm. We might need to work on that.' HT smiles kindly and pats me on the head.

And picks something out. The twig, that sign of university-level swim knowledge, has got stuck in my swim cap.

I've played in thousands of concerts over the years, including the BBC Proms (a surprisingly small stage, considering it's such a big one), a Rossini opera in the Highlands of Scotland (who needs opera costumes when you have kilts?), to the descendants of General Bhutto in Pakistan (they were so close they were literally standing on my toe), Haydn in a tractor shed in Victoria (seriously *the* best acoustic ever), at the Russian embassy in Kabul (so much vodka) and at the Handover in Hong Kong in 1997 (I swear I saw Tony Blair cry). I've played for royalty, people experiencing homelessness, gazillionaires and screaming babies. I don't have a single favourite concert, but I do have a favourite type of concert, and that is always the one where I was playing out of compassion and kindness.

In 2011 Queensland experienced the worst floods in living memory. Thirty-three people are known to have died, hundreds of thousands were affected and billions of dollars of damage was done. I was living in Sydney at the time but was so moved by the sight of people digging endless mud from their homes that I took my viola onto the streets of Sydney and busked for the flood recovery fund. I hadn't practised for years (don't tell my students!) so I kept the repertoire as simple as I could: some Bach, a bit more Bach, a few songs and some Bach. I was fortunate that I could announce where I was playing on ABC Radio, so dozens of people showed up each day in various spots around the city. For one of these concerts I played in a park in the inner-city suburb of Glebe. I set up underneath an enormous Moreton Bay fig tree, opened my case for donations, and started to play the song *When I Am Laid in Earth* by Henry Purcell. After some solitary notes, the audience started to sing, very softly. When the volume had grown to support them enough, people began to let rip and sing with full operatic voices. It was completely unexpected. There we were, all strangers, and through a disaster we had come together; we held kindness and music in our hearts, and together it became the perfect concert. And at the end, a small, bright-eyed woman came up and asked me a simple question about where I was born. It was a meeting that would change my life.

The bright-eyed woman was Charlie.

Just as life vibrates better with an open heart, so does the sound we create on our instruments. String instruments have, at their heart, a tiny piece of wood that transfers the vibrations of the strings down from the bridge to the back of the instrument, the main vibrating area. The position of this tiny stick dictates the quality of sound of the instrument, whether it is muscular and balanced or weak and unstable. Move it less than a millimetre and the sound completely changes. In English the stick is called the soundpost, but the French call it by its true name: *âme*, or soul.

There's an expression from Indonesia that when a person is not integrated with themselves, is not at one with themselves, their front and back are far apart. A string instrument is the same. If the front and back don't speak to each other, the instrument will always sound frail and undeveloped. For our musical soul to be congruent, all around it needs to come together: the player must stimulate the strings with control and freedom, the wood of the instrument must be ready to vibrate by being mature and clear, the parts must be perfectly shaped and fitted together so no gap is left, the strings must be fresh and lively, and, most crucially, the body of the musician and the instrument must work as one being.

As my swimming coach Helentherese says, 'The kindness of playing is that it keeps us humble. The start of each note is built on so many variables – bow weight, sound point, bow speed, not to mention the placing of the left-hand fingers to the nearest hundredth of a millimetre to sit in the centre of the note's intonation (itself dependent on the key of the piece) – that no-one can ever *really* know exactly how it will come out on the day. Of course, we practise so we have a good idea, but still … The unknowing, the fuzziness is a metaphor for life. We can't control everything. We just have to work hard, have integrity in our learning, and then go for it. Sometimes there'll be a disaster (like the wind blowing my bow off the string at the funeral yesterday) but generally it works out.'

———————————————

Coppicing is an ancient practice, dating back to at least 10,000 BCE. Young trees are felled and the new growth from the stump, or stool, is then periodically cut back and used for building, fencing, firewood, charcoal. Coppicing was the most common way of harvesting wood before big machines made transporting whole trees far too easy. Once the tree is coppiced (or pollarded, if it's cut a bit higher up), the tree will live longer than if it isn't coppiced, and the sunlight the coppicing allows brings air and butterflies and diverse wildlife to the space. Coppiced trees are a very efficient way of making a hedge, or a windbreak along a paddock's edge.

Music practice, for me, is a coppice. We take a piece of music, the tree, and we take it apart to allow it to grow in our own imagination and will. We give ourselves time, light, and space to hear ourselves properly. And when we have taken the piece as our own, rather than a facsimile of someone else's performance, then we are free and we can re-create our interpretation a thousand times, each one unique and new. Our coppice provides a hedgerow of safety, behind which we shelter from mediocrity.

———————————————

There are pieces musicians play thousands of times, and some we play just once. And there are pieces musicians wish we could play a thousand times, and some we hope we will play only once. Those hopes and pieces do not always align, but when they do it is a feeling of pure fulfilment.

A work I have played only once, but would love to again, is Dvořák's sixth symphony. His New World Symphony, the ninth, is very popular and deservedly so, but this sixth gem is a little undervalued. Because, like so many other composers, Dvořák was a viola player, the viola parts in this symphony, and all his music, sing with desire and ability. They are simply a joy to play. They make sense, not only musically but physically. Dvořák worked as a viola player for many years – in a dance band in Bohemia, and with orchestras in Prague – and he believed if a piece was to sing fully, all the parts needed to be written with that instrument in mind, not just as a filler for the harmony. So when you play Dvořák's music, the viola sings with your body because of the setting of the notes on the instrument, the way they lie in your hand. Mozart, also a viola player, does the same thing. There is a deep satisfaction playing this music, a real feeling your viola and you are being given the very best chance to succeed, and you don't have to make any effort. The sound comes from an easy place. Ease, joy and glory.

I have been studying a book by Philip Farkas, a horn god and the principal of the Chicago Symphony Orchestra among others, who wrote a book called *The Art of French Horn Playing*. This is considered by many to be the horn bible (well, he was a god), and includes much gloriously nerdy information about things like embouchure (including slightly disturbing pictures of players' embouchures on an open ring), repertoire, warmups, developing range, sound and how to practise. Speaking of practice, Farkas himself practised his horn every single day until he died, aged seventy-eight. I was reading his bible the other day and was particularly taken with a passage about sound production. As I mentioned before when my lips turned blue, it is very easy to press too hard with the horn on your embouchure. It can give false stability and you then don't work how you should, on the whole embouchure. Farkas recommended holding the horn without putting your little finger around the hook, so your left hand, which uses the valves, does not have any anchor to press the mouthpiece into the face. As Farkas said, if you're pressing, the sound is coming from your left bicep, not from your diaphragm. I was struck by this simple yet profound advice. Our sound needs to come from the right place. If it doesn't, we simply cannot sustain it. We hit a false note and lose integrity and congruency. If our sound comes from our bicep, we will always be fighting. If it comes from our centre, our path will be clear.

As you read before, every sound has a fundamental note, then a series of overtones spiralling up into the ether. It is the balance of those overtones that allows us to differentiate a cello from a clarinet from a child's voice from a lion's roar. Depending on the key, or which home note the composer uses, each instrument (well, not so much the lions) is going to have a different balance of overtones to supplement the fundamental note. For instance, on the viola and cello our bottom string is C, so any piece in the key of C major or C minor is going to stimulate the open strings as earlier overtones. So it is going to be easier to mould a piece in C than a piece in C sharp, as the open string notes for C sharp would be much higher up the harmonic series and won't have so much influence over the sound. In the hands of a skilled musician, all music, no matter the key, will sound gorgeous and fully crafted, but the musician will have to work much harder to achieve that resonance in some keys. Historically, different keys elicited different emotions from the musician and the listener: D major was for celebrations, F major for grounding and calm, C minor for love's laments, C major for innocence. With true intonation, not the tempered pitch where the piano is imprisoned, each key brings a whole different set of overtones, and those overtones, subtly, oh so subtly, affect the way we bring music into our hearts. And the more we listen, the more we allow the music to enter. As they learn, baby cellists or viola players only play in certain keys for a while, so the feeling of resonance supports them during their music nursery years. And on the horn, in my own music nursery, I am also playing in the most basic of keys; because I'm playing a horn with the fundamental note of F, I am playing in the keys that match it best – F and C and maybe B flat on a good day. If Peter gave me a piece in a far-off key, I'd probably cry. Well, I might complain a bit.

Instruments have a key they vibrate best in. We have a hormone we vibrate best in. As the years go by and the testosterone in my body does its work, I feel, finally, I am playing in the right key. All those years of being oestrogen-based, for me, did not stimulate my true fundamental note. I was playing in C sharp, not in C. Distant overtones took over and I felt no resonance in my being or the way I went through life. Everything, everything, was a struggle. As the key changes with my fundamental hormone, I feel the reverberations gather force, I feel an inner kindness, and the distant overtones fade and surrender.

And now I feel my resonance sing.

No one can really know himself,
detach himself from his inner being.
Yet, each day he must put to the test,
What is in the end, clear.
What he is and what he was,
what he can be and what he might be.

JOHANN WOLFGANG VON GOETHE

I believe our approach to music, whether listening or learning or playing, reveals how kind we are with ourselves. If we practise and play with honesty, we are kind to ourselves and our audience and the music. The kindness we show by offering our devotion to music is returned to us tenfold. Each day, musicians put themselves to the test with their practice, and each day a musician shows who they are, and who they can be. And each day they imagine what they might be.

At music college all those years ago, I remember another student commenting on the skills of different students. Music colleges are very competitive places, and people are constantly being judged on their playing. I remember this student, Richard, admiring a clarinettist, Dov, for his skill. But it wasn't only his playing skill, it was his practice skills. Richard said he would stand outside Dov's practice room and listen to his practice, so that he could copy it in his own cello playing. Because Dov practised with humility and kindness and honesty. He did not simply play through his music as I did at that time, he took the music apart, building it note by note, phrase by phrase, until the entire structure was understood and commanded. Dov was an engineer, making his own music machine. Nothing now could shake him. Dov had taught himself patience through music.

But not only patience; music is a reminder of our brief existence on earth. Music is practised for so many hours – one piece can take a thousand hours to properly have in your mind and body, and that's not even considering the time it takes to reach the level where you can begin that piece. So with music like Bartók's Viola Concerto (one of the hardest pieces for viola), it takes ten years to achieve the level where you can play it, twenty minutes to perform it and then, whoosh, it's gone. Where did it go? Where did our life go? Where do we hold our impressions of our music and our memories? How do we remember, except sing? How can we do anything except be kind to ourselves and accept the brevity of music, and our lives?

Yet, despite its own fleeting existence, music unmasks reality with every sound and every silence. Each note is a seed, holding the potential for all direction, all decision, all emotion.

For years I ran away from playing music, despite the kindness it bestowed on me. My viola had taken me from a deeply unhappy childhood to the leading conservatoires and concert halls of the world, and yet I turned my back on playing because I could not be kind to myself. I could not forgive myself for being transgender. And now, I cannot wait to play. I run towards music and know its kindness is forgiveness. It is never too late to start, and it is never too late to return.

E:
WISDOM

Music is your own experience, your thoughts, your wisdom. If you don't live it, it won't come out of your horn.

CHARLIE PARKER

———————————

I FIND MYSELF STAGGERED, still, at the simplicity, clarity and humility of all my music teachers, beginning with the unflinching love of Simon Stace, my viola teacher at high school in Shrewsbury, and continuing to music college in the 1980s. England had a symphony of musicians seek refuge before and during the Second World War, and I was at college just as these gurus were retiring. My college days were illustrated by men from central Europe: the Amadeus Quartet, all but one from Vienna; Eli Goren, leader of the BBC Symphony Orchestra, also from Vienna; Milan Škampa, viola player of the Smetana Quartet, from Prague; and William Pleeth, teacher of Jacqueline du Pré, his parents from central Europe and he from central London.

To a man, every single one of these musicians played. They did not work at their music, they did not strain and stress, they took their instruments and their music and they played with them like a juggler with fire sticks, tossing them and catching them and, yes, sometimes dropping them but never flinching and playing on and on until the music was filled with rapture and energy. To a man, these teachers, many of them in their seventies and eighties, were exquisitely youthful. It wasn't the youth of their bodies (although Milan Škampa did beat me in a race up the stairs when he was in his sixties and I was barely twenty), it was the youth of their curiosity, imagination and lack of assumption. These men, particularly the men from Vienna, had lost family members and any assumption of safety, they had had to leave behind the holdalls of their life to reach safety, and the only thing they could keep was their music. And still, it was always about play. As Norbert Brainin, violinist of the Amadeus Quartet, would remind me, we play an instrument, we don't work it.

As my college years went on, my cohort fractured into the people who did a lot of practice, and by that I mean eight hours a day, people who did a respectable amount, around three or four hours (me on a good day), and people who did virtually nothing. The latter students did not last. At the end of each year, student numbers were whittled away by – what? Laziness? Confusion? Self-doubt? One viola player, a guy called Jonathan, hardly ever practised, but when he did he played us all into the ground. He was kicked out and became a boat builder.

What became clear, apart from the hours we spent in practice rooms, was that the people who did the most amount of practice were not necessarily the most interesting players to listen to. And it was for a simple reason – they did nothing beyond their music. To do eight hours practice takes about ten hours, as you can only really concentrate for an hour at a time, then have a break, spot of lunch, pint of beer, etc. Add to that your academic work, and the proverb 'all work and no play makes Jack a dull boy' proved true. As the years went by at college, I tried all the ways of practice. For a few months I even did the whole eight-hour thing, but the amount that worked best was definitely the middle way – three or four hours, which gave me time to read, go to concerts, generally play up and grow up.

As my quartet and I worked our way into playing our music, we received nothing but encouragement from our teachers. They would get frustrated, of course, and sometimes even stamp their feet. How exasperating for them to witness four young people interpret music they had played for decades and knew from every perspective; we were mere musical puppies for them. Imagine Patrick White teaching your teenager creative writing. Or Sidney Nolan taking an adult art class. It takes a very special teacher, like Peter, to embrace the different levels of learning.

One day my quartet was invited to Sir Michael Tippett's hotel room in Manchester to play for him. He was in his eighties by then, tall, stooped, thin and still dark-haired, a man with a reputation of sternness and of commitment to his beliefs. During the Second World War, Tippett had refused to join the military in any form, even as a non-combatant, and had been imprisoned for three months in Wormwood Scrubs prison. The day he was released, a month early, he went straight to a concert and heard a performance of his String Quartet No. 2, the piece we would be playing for him.

Tippett's music, like the man himself, had a reputation for being difficult. His second symphony was so technically challenging that, in a live broadcast of it, the orchestra had had to stop and regroup. (I had played one of his symphonies at college and felt at risk of failing from beginning to end.) So when our quartet went to this great and scary composer's hotel room, we were not confident. We had only started learning the quartet recently, and it was a language of music we had not experienced before, a new dialect with strange cadence and stress. The phrases were uneven and awkward, the articulation intangible and mysterious, and the harmonies foggy and angry. The anger is no surprise, considering the background of the piece: Tippett had the inspiration for the main theme after the Munich Conference and appeasement of Hitler, and despite Tippett being a pacifist, the news of how much had been given up clearly left him disturbed. The music pulls you in with a sweet air, but it's the sweetness of someone who ultimately wishes you harm. Before long the music is swilling in anger, regret and dysfunction, as if the four instruments are fighting each other all the way through.

As my quartet played, at a certain point Sir Michael became frustrated with one of the other player's articulation, and the composer pointed at me, still female-bodied, stamped his foot, and shouted to the others, 'No! Do it like him!'

This was a clear lesson in the impotence of getting angry. From that moment, we both lost our respect for the man as our teacher, but we also became so worried he would explode again that we lost the vigour in our playing. His lack of control had only diminished him, and he looked ashamed after his outburst. We left, feeling perhaps a little humiliated, and played the piece only once again. Sir Michael had transgressed a law of teaching: to highlight an issue with only positive attention, and not to take an easier, cynical path by diminishing and mocking players. He had forgotten to play.

――――――――――――

'You just need one good note, just one!'

Peter Luff, after I had played one good note. It was a D, second line down treble clef, if you're interested.

'Playing horn is like playing golf: you just need one good shot to keep you coming back.'

And with that I try to play the D again and it has disappeared, a shy platypus in the harmonic pond of life.

Things have been progressing with the horn in the usual way of things progressing with the horn, that is, two steps forward, one and a half steps backwards. Still, if you take enough steps, those half steps each day begin to add up and I feel so bold as to ask Peter if I can take an exam.

He looks at me, twinkle and serious assessment in equal store. I wonder whether he is going to say grade one or two, so I am dangerously flattered when he says, 'Sure! You need to for your book, right? Have a look at grade four.'

Oh yes! Grade four! The last time I took a grade four exam I was in primary school, I think Year 5, and I felt supremely advanced and brilliant. And now, in year fifty-four, I feel even more supremely advanced and brilliant. I couldn't be prouder. I race home and tell Charlie, who is about to start a meditation with her online group and asks me to go upstairs if I'm going to be noisy. I am going to be noisy. I have already bought the exam music and I pull it out, flick through it and pounce on a real favourite: *Che Farò Senza Euridice?* (*What Will I Do Without Euridice?*), from Gluck's opera *Orfeo ed Euridice*.

This heartbreaking aria describes the moment Orfeo kills Euridice by looking back at her (well, he was warned), and now he is trying to fathom what he will do without her. I look through the music to see if there are any of my dreaded Gs and there are not. The highest note is E, but there are a lot of them. I pick up my horn (top tip: leave your instrument in a safe place with a cloth over it, that way you don't have to keep unpacking it) and ride up and down a few elevators before diving into the Gluck.

Oh dear. Poor Charlie. Her equanimity is certainly being tested in this, my first outing into Hades. Still, I make it across the Styx, just, definitely and many times kill Euridice, not only with my look but also with a few teetering Es, and feel my work is done. Time for a whisky.

I present my work (I did practise it a few more times) to Peter in the next lesson.

'Ah yes, everyone likes to play this. It's wonderful for the horn. Okay, let's hear you.'

I start off, and not too bad. My sound has gone from tractor to lawn mower, so slightly less agricultural, but still with whiffs of pasture and the occasional manure. I get through the first few phrases with only the odd bung note, and then reach a terrifying precipice of notes going up, not down. It is the musical equivalent of one of those parkour leaps from building to building, except you've only just started training and you don't have your stretchy trousers on.

I head into the phrase, trying to garner support from my diaphragm like a politician from an unruly mob. I fail. Spectacularly. The leap ends up with my ankle broken and the ledge high above me, unconquered.

Peter picks me up, dusts me off and asks a simple question.

'So why did that happen?'

I feel he should have asked why *didn't* that happen, but I mutter something about support this and diaphragm that, then he nods sagely and I try again.

Thought precedes form: right thought, right action. The horn, beyond any other instrument, demands that you are right here, right now, nowhere else, not in the future looking forward to the next phrase, not in the past lamenting a missed note, but only here, here, here ... Each note, each moment, your only space. Peter sums it up: 'The only time I feel completely in the moment is when I'm playing the horn.'

This time I really concentrate, rather than think I'm concentrating, and it works. I fly up from G to an E and feel there might be room for even more height, an Olympic pole vaulter on the up and up.

I continue my journey back and forth across the Styx, either dying a very noisy death or coming back to life with a lower note, until – *danger*. I skid to a halt, a musical incarnation of the roadrunner when the road disappears beneath his still-spinning legs. After a series of rests, my next note is a high(ish) E. It's the top of my current range and it is a vertigo-inducing, knee-shaking, spirit-defining entry.

I take a deep breath. Good start, although I note there is no sign of an abdominal six-pack, unless you count my stomach looking like I've been drinking a six-pack a day for a while. I release my breath and hurtle from where I hope the note is, a parachutist waiting for said parachute to open.

It does not. I die an ignominious musical death.

It is a miracle that Peter does not wince or take out some noise-cancelling headphones. He smiles his Buddha smile and says the most beautiful thing.

'Ed, imagine the music is already there. It's flowing past you, and all you need to do is step into the river of music.'

Peter's words remind me of a similar evocation from Sir Edward Elgar, English composer of such masterpieces as his Cello Concerto, Symphony No. 1, and Violin Concerto: 'My idea is that there is music in the air, music all around us, the world is full of it and you simply take as much as you require.' Which in turn reminds me of a quote from Hermann Hesse's *Siddhartha*: 'When Siddhartha listened attentively to this river, to the song of a thousand voices; when he did not listen to the sorrow or laughter, when he did not bind his soul to any one particular voice and absorb it in his Self, but heard them all, the whole, the unity; then the great song of a thousand voices consisted of one word: Om – perfection.'

I throw all my assumptions and fears and desires aside, and I step into the river of music.

Zoltán Kodály was a Hungarian composer who created music woven with silver and gold, sapphires and diamonds, earth and rock. His music was a blend of ancient song and modern composing techniques, a kind of atavistic modernism. In the first half of the twentieth century, Kodály spent years travelling central Europe – Hungary, Romania, Bulgaria, Czechoslovakia – and recording folk songs on a huge, and presumably very heavy, wax cylinder. What would he think looking at our compact recording equipment today? Kodály turned those folk songs into some of the great works of the early twentieth century: the opera Háry János, the orchestral work Dances from Galánta, a solo cello sonata, and a song that translates as *See the Gypsies Munching Cheese*, a favourite if you're hungry.

Kodály's influence lives on today in our music classrooms: we learn rhythm through his development of rhythm words (ta, ti-ti, tikka-tikka), we sing with his adopted Curwen hand symbols for each degree (note) of the scale (a closed fist for the first or tonic note, an open palm for the fifth or dominant, etc.), and we learn those notes in an order based on the child's natural growth (the tonic and sixth or submediant first). Kodály believed a child's knowledge of fine music was as important as their knowledge of their mother tongue and should be taught in a similar way. He also believed music should be demonstrated with works by the finest composers, and then the child would continue to seek that level of artistry. If you play music that only uses a few chords and is poorly played or sung, the child will only ever expect the same. Kodály believed in the universal right of every child, and therefore every adult, to be musically literate and to have access to structured, experiential music training, not simply listening to distant lectures. To do, to sing and to play was at the heart of his teaching. And to sing and play folk songs was the beginning. If we play the folk songs of our language, music makes sense from that lived and spoken perspective.

Before Kodály went walking with his wax cylinder he had a more European, generic style of composing. That doesn't sound so compelling, but one of his most-loved works comes from this period, his Adagio for violin and piano.

Adagio is a tricky word for musicians. Whenever we see it we are tempted to think 'ooh, slow' and stop there. But adagio's true meaning is to take care, go gently, don't rush. Kodály composed this nine-minute piece for violin and piano but quickly transcribed it for viola, then cello and double bass.

You remember we talked earlier in the book, way back there, about the harmonic series, and the overtones? And that the first overtone of a fundamental note is simply the same note, up an octave, then we have a fifth and we go back to another octave? Kodály makes use of that ladder with this piece. We start on the lowest note on the viola with such a long, tautly spread tune that you feel either the viola or your heart will not be able to stand the weight. Then again, the same melody an octave higher. The weight increases and it becomes intolerable. Now Kodály lifts us to that fifth overtone as our home note, and the light dapples and relents. You feel you have escaped the unfaceable, but once more, from the light, we are pulled back. And just when you think you cannot take any more exposure to life, to this great and mysterious happiness and sadness in one, the octave is pushed up for the last time, straining at the very top of the instrument.

It is an astonishing piece to witness. And to play, it tests every part of your nerve because it is so extended, to the point of being distorted. The whole notes, the long notes, reach beyond the horizon and you must hold your nerve, knowing their end will come. Long notes can be the hardest to play, as they can seem either empty and idle, or the opposite – so full of life, you never want them to end. The keen beginner always rushes through them, wanting to get to a faster bit, a bit they can feel comfortable with in the movement, and the competent amateur holds them for too long, thinking the deliberation makes them even more profound. Whole notes show us where we are going, or where we're not. They illuminate what is true inside us, how strong our inner pulse is and if it will withstand the waiting. As a string player you need to ration your bow, as a wind or brass player you need to ration your breath. You must assess, relax and trust yourself. You must be in the river.

As we learn music, we assimilate pulse, then rhythm, and once they are fully acknowledged, we learn metre. Metre is the division of music into groups. It is visual – bars and bar lines (Americans call them measures and measure lines) – and it is aural. Think of the difference between a march and a waltz. A march has four beats in each group or bar of notes, a waltz has three. The best way to know how many beats there are in a bar is to count out loud – can you count four over a waltz beat? Or three for a march? It feels odd, doesn't it? When you count the correct number, you quickly hear and feel how the beat, or pulse, slots in with the music, or the music slots in with the pulse. Once again, we learn through doing, not reading. When people are reading music for the first time, the bar lines can seem limiting, like bars on a prison window. How can the music get through without pausing a little? We advance and the bar lines become shadows of the beat, giving relief to its light, giving us something to swing off rather than tie our horse to.

Playing music takes us beyond the limitations of time to another clock, another metre, the metre of memory. We hold in our bodies, just as Kodály said, the feeling of the music. We hold in our bodies where the pulse is, where the stress is, and we know at the beginning of each note how it will end. We begin the music, but once each note is begun, we must let it die for the next one to form. Music in its flow is the acceptance of life, decline and death, without question.

Music lives in its own dimension, and the time we measure our lives by becomes superfluous. I have been in rehearsals or my own practice where the time of hours and seconds stands to one side, secondary now to the time of the pulse. When that happens, you truly shift universes. You are yourself. No, you are beyond yourself – you are living measure for measure and you are letting go, from note to note.

───────────

If you have spent your whole life training to be a musician, there can be times when music begins to lose its meaning. Just like wearing out a memory, or a photograph, or a word, music can cease to hold any significance in your life, especially if it's not being supported by other loves. It's not just music losing its meaning, *playing* music loses its meaning, as if a child has lost the desire to play. The world breaks a little.

I have come close to giving up music twice: when I was thirteen (teenage hormones) and my mum wouldn't let me (thanks, Mum), and when I was twenty-three, studying at the Royal Academy of Music in London, when my viola teacher John White also wouldn't let me (thanks, Professor White).

My quartet had won a scholarship to study with the three surviving members of the Amadeus Quartet – Norbert Brainin, Siegmund Nissel, and Martin Lovett. It was a difficult time: we had moved to London from the safety of Manchester; from knowing everyone at college we didn't know anyone at college; we had the pressures of the profession right in front of us instead of years away, and keeping a quartet together is precarious. All these stresses meant my playing began to collapse. I would drag myself into rehearsals, drag myself to practise on my own, but the essential desire to make music had run away. I was a viola player with no play. It was a disastrous year for the quartet and we broke up. I had nothing to look forward to after college except scrabbling for freelance gigs in London, and in my last lesson of that year with Professor White I told him I was thinking of giving up. All year I had felt our relationship was a little cool, but in this lesson Professor White showed all the wisdom of his decades of teaching.

John White had come from the best viola lineage: he had had lessons with Watson Forbes and Lionel Tertis, the man who showed how virtuosic the viola could be and had inspired William Walton to write his viola concerto. John White might not have had to escape the Nazis, but his own background was certainly not privileged. His dad was a miner in Yorkshire and played the violin, so John learnt as a boy and eventually fell in love with the viola. He went on to found the Alberni Quartet and became a leading viola player and teacher in England. I was lucky to have him as a teacher, but I didn't realise it then. I do now.

John White looked me sternly in the eye and asked what I was going to do if I didn't play the viola. I muttered something about going travelling, and he grabbed a piece of paper and a pencil and made me write down, there and then, the pros and cons of playing the viola. At the top of my pros (I don't remember what the cons were) I put 'travel'. He didn't need to say anything else. If that is what I wanted, the viola would give it to me. I was literally holding my future in my hands.

What do you want to say? How can it get any better than this? What do you really mean? Who are you? All these questions are answered by music, and my questions were, and always will be, answered by my instrument, the viola.

———————————————

I continued to play and stepped into a run of failures. Just because I had decided to keep music, I had to prove myself to music for it to keep me. I failed auditions for orchestras and teachers, and music kept beating me over the head until finally I practised enough, wanted it enough, and I won a job with the English String Orchestra, then with the Hong Kong Philharmonic. I embrace my failures now and see them as a necessary step in life, but at the time they almost derailed me again. It wasn't until I took responsibility for my own playing, my own practice, my own approach to music, my own life, that I moved forward. I celebrated what I could do, worked at what I couldn't, and accepted the responsibility of being a musician.

As the months and years go by since my first testosterone shot, I see the possibilities, the impossibilities and the realities of fulfilling my maleness. Some things changed so quickly, some things seemed to never shift at all. The physical changes leapt ahead in the first year, then seemed to stall and even reverse. There were days I would wake up and forget I was ever anything other than male, and days I would wake and be back in my old skin – trapped, empty, pointless. With every tiny metamorphosis forensically examined, how could my life go on like this? Existence under your own microscope is not easy. I was a pedantic teacher of myself, stopping at every note, never allowing the phrase to flow, never allowing the bow to reach the end, always checking, stopping, judging.

I went to a party with Charlie. A woman I hardly knew, although she obviously knew my story, leant over and said, 'Ed, darling, so how *are* you?' with a patronising smile, clearly expecting some juicy details of the life of a transgender man. The truth is, there are no juicy details. Being transgender generally sucks, but you learn to live with it, and, in the end, days can go by when you forget. You get dressed, you work, you eat, you occasionally forget to book your next hormone shot so you feel crap for a few days, then the whole cycle begins again. Transitioning is a lifesaver for me and thousands of others, but it only goes so far. If you haven't done your practice, the music fails. If you haven't accepted the realities of being trans, you will fail. Dr Bearman warned me about the power of testosterone and needing to use my muscles, and I have also learnt to temper the power of my expectation. I wanted so much, but no-one knows how they will react to their new hormones, especially in their fifties. Will our face masculinise? Will our shoulders broaden and our fat distribution change? Will our voices deepen? Will our muscles gain heft?

But beyond all that, where will our self go? What kind of man do I want to be? From my own family, my father's example was of a man who created an adventurous life – sailing around the world in the merchant navy, working in Nigeria in the 1960s, moving to Singapore after his divorce – but is the mark of a man what he does for himself or what he does for others? And isn't that the case for any gender? Beside his adventures, my father also left behind an ex-wife and four children in a small house in the middle of England. My dad could sail a yacht in the toughest races in the world, but he couldn't face the most important job of all, supporting his children. So, I could look at my dad and wonder if I would look like him, but I refuse the example he provides of masculinity. I follow my mother's example of humanity, not my father's, as a base for my own moral code. And the same with music. The early stage of becoming a musician is to copy other players, then we mature and develop and create our own voice. Ultimately, we need to make our own performance, not copy someone else's recording.

And it is a performance no-one else can imagine.

Recently, I was asked to appear on a television show and contribute to a discussion about a cis (natural-born) male writer who had written a novel with a transgender girl at its heart. The novel was written from her perspective, in the first person.

The TV producer who called me said I would be asked my opinion of non-transgender people writing about transgender issues; they wanted me to appear because I am transgender and a writer. Ironically, I was writing this book, so amid discussing bravery and resilience through learning music, three viola students waiting outside for their lessons and a national radio show on the weekend, I didn't have time to add a TV show to the list.

But the subject has weighed heavily on me since then, even if it's fundamentally simple.

Some of my favourite books were written by people imagining worlds beyond their own. It would be ridiculous to demand the end to imagination and to ban writers from creating anything other than their own lived experience. You may as well ban books.

But when there is an outcry, writers, often straight, often white, often middle-aged and middle class, reply, 'Well, no-one is stopping transgender people writing their own stories. What's the problem?'

That's a good question. There is a problem, and not just for transgender people. There's a problem for anyone who hasn't had space and quiet to reflect, money to support them, time and energy to write, the confidence to write, the education to write. When you throw into that mix a significant amount of time dealing with the regular, often invasive, treatment of transgender symptoms, and dealing with enduring societal hatred and prejudice, writing a 70,000-word novel isn't exactly first on our to-do list. Forgive us if we concentrate on not committing suicide first.

But if you do, as a cis person, decide that there is really absolutely nothing else to write about, and you decide to describe a world that must be fully experienced to be fully understood, perhaps you could do us transgender folk a favour and write truthfully about us.

Because being transgender is not a drama, as many writers suggest, it is not a terror to sit beside drugs and abuse, we are not victims, we are not 'other', and we are not creatures to be examined through the bars of a cage. When we are treated respectfully and properly and given a chance to get on with our lives, we are just regular folk. We are teachers, we are firefighters, we are doctors, nurses, police, politicians, civil servants, farm workers – we are anyone.

I hope this is the last of it. People making money from our lives. I hope privileged cis writers will do one simple thing: stop stealing our stories. Because our reality is something that imagination alone can never capture.

I admit, there were times when I felt transitioning wouldn't be enough for me, that living as a transgender man was simply too difficult, too torn, and I wanted to give up. But Charlie was always there, lifting me up when I fell, reminding me of what I might be. Charlie didn't give up. She reminded me that, just like my viola playing, I had to accept who I was becoming and remember my true nature. I would never be a natural-born male, and being a transgender male was a strength known only to very few. My maleness had survived a lifetime of oestrogen, and not many men could say that.

A viola is not a big violin, a small cello, or just a joke. It is its own voice. It is a viola. And a trans man is not a lesser man, a masculine woman or a mental illness. I am a centaur, and how fucking cool is that.

———————————

Since I play both the viola and the cello, sometimes I like to play the same piece on the two different instruments to feel how the character of the piece changes with each voice. The viola is tuned an octave higher than the cello, but the cello can easily play at the same pitch as the viola, so what makes those sounds distinct? Are there pieces that would only work on one instrument, or is transposing music an opportunity to hear the same message with a new accent?

A piece I often turn to in times of sadness is Bach's second cello suite, in the key of D minor. I studied this on viola at college and played it for successful auditions, so it has always felt like a dear, trusted friend. Bach wrote six cello suites, and each one has a distinct character. The first suite is the most famous, with its skipping and larking around, but in the second suite the light turns muted and the mood uncertain and full of self-doubt. The prelude has a subtle sway to it and brings to mind an artwork by Bill Viola, an American video artist whose work *Passage Into Night* is displayed at the National Gallery in Canberra. In the video a figure walks, endlessly. They are swaddled in robes and it is impossible to know whether they are male or female, or if they are walking towards the camera, or away from it. The light in the video shimmers, each atom burning heat from the earth, and the figure walks on, leaving and returning eternally.

When I play the prelude of the Bach on the viola, each rise and fall of the music leads my fingers to a new idea of the destination. The music plays me, and all I need to do is submit and allow it to flow. The music takes me where it wants, a wheel moving up and forwards, even when it is going down and backwards.

In recent years I have played the same piece on the cello, and naturally it feels quite different. The weight and balance of the shorter cello bow and the thickness of the strings held the music back initially, but as I became used to the need for more muscularity in its playing, and to be bolder in my physicality, I understand now that the music is the same. As the run of notes chase each other out to the end of the pier, the feeling once you get there is the same. You do not want to jump from the pier, you want to step back into safety and return to your home. And once you've reached the end, the celebrations are tempered by the knowledge of what it has taken to get there. The desperation has gone, replaced by integration. Arvo Pärt says it best:

> The highest virtue of music, for me, lies outside of its mere sound. The particular timbre of an instrument is part of the music, but it is not the most important element. If it were, I would be surrendering to the essence of the music. Music must exist of itself … two, three notes … the essence must be there, independent of the instruments.

The meaning is the same, the desire is the same, all that has changed is the messenger.

_____

Young cello-playing Rosie has come so far already, and only half the year has gone by. In her latest lesson, I ask Rosie if she would like to learn a new piece, and as she sits embracing her cello, she gives a superb answer.

'No, I think I'll stick with this one. I think I need to get it a bit better before I learn something new.'

I admit, as a teacher I sometimes give my students new pieces too soon. Just like holding whole notes takes courage, so does keeping a student on a piece they might be growing bored, frustrated or fed up with. When Rosie says she wants to perfect the piece she is playing, *Go Tell Aunt Rhody*, I am relieved and delighted. Rosie has already learnt a crucial lesson: it takes time to develop something, anything, and the longer we can delay moving on, the more pleasure we can have from the details of life. As Dr Suzuki teaches, patience is a lack of expectation. Rosie has added to that. Patience is an exploration of process.

Go Tell Aunt Rhody is an American folk song that originated in an opera by Jean-Jacques Rousseau, the writer, philosopher and composer. It's massively gratifying that such an important piece of string pedagogy was composed by such a giant of educational philosophy. Rousseau believed a child should have as natural an upbringing as possible and be encouraged to develop their compassion and confidence through self-discovery, rather than being dictated to by teachers. His philosophy matches well with Kodály's, and Rosie has shown how successfully this method can work by taking clear charge of her own progress.

Anyway, back to *Go Tell Aunt Rhody*. It's a music sandwich, like *Twinkle, Twinkle, Little Star*, so in ternary form, which makes it easier to memorise, and it is the first piece students learn where there is an ambiguity in the emotion. We are asked in the lyrics to go tell Aunt Rhody her old grey goose is dead, yet the music suggests a mood more of practicality: perhaps now it's dead they can eat it, or they are happy because it won't chase them in the garden anymore. It's open to interpretation and students love telling their own story, mixing the good and the bad, the delicious and the morbid. Since Rosie learnt *Twinkle,* her playing has developed and she can now play with varied dynamics and make her phrases grow or diminish, crescendo or diminuendo. She has expanded the use of her bow and now plays with a variety of articulations: very short, quick notes, short notes with spaces, and now long notes leaning into the next note as closely as possible. This is called legato or smooth bowing, and it's an extraordinary challenge.

The bow goes in two directions – up and down, or as I prefer to say, pull and push. The way a musician presents music, the articulation, is infinite, and often we want to have a certain edge and roughness to our sound with the pull and push. The endless challenge of the string player when we want to play legato is to try to eliminate any gap in the sound as we change the direction of the bow. What often happens as we approach the end of the bow is that we slow down, tighten our hold of the bow, and the change in direction makes a bump in the music. The flow is lost and the phrase needs to start all over again. To play smoothly, we need to keep the bow moving at the same speed and relax the bowhold a little, so the bow can change direction of its own accord rather than being controlled. If we can keep the fingers supple, they act like shock absorbers and are able to suck up any bump in the sound. The equivalent to bow changes for wind and brass players is to take breaths, but they often delay the breath to the start of the next phrase so it is not obvious. String players need to change bow much more often than that, but since our bow is our breath, we try to sound like wind or brass players by tricking our brains.

Imagine a racetrack. If you are standing at the same height as the people running around the track, it looks from your perspective as if they are running back and forth. But if you raise your perspective and look down on the people, you see now they are running in an oval. That's what we imagine as we change our bow, the running in an endless loop. It's not necessarily a concept I would introduce to a young student, so Rosie and I work on closing our eyes, listening and hearing if we are playing with any holes. The player with the fewer holes after a phrase wins. I start, and as I turn from a pull bow to a push, I forget my imagery and there's a big gap in my sound. Rosie plays, and I ask her to keep her arm moving at the same speed and to imagine she is spreading butter with her bow on the toast of her string. It works. She wins.

I love it when my students are better than me. Especially when they are seven years old.

———————————

I must finish what I've started,
even if, inevitably, what I finish turns
out not to be what I began.

SALMAN RUSHDIE

———————————

When musicians prepare music for performance, there is an idea of the end at the beginning, just like architects thinking of the roof in the foundations of a building. But who knows what will happen along the way?

How do you start a piece? Is it with a feeling of breathing out, or a gasp of surprise and energy? Is it with an explosion of movement, or must you temper the attack with your intent? Where does the phrase go? What is the most important note in this phrase, and where is the lowest point? How will this phrase link to the next? Does it make sense? Does it need to make sense? Or will it be more arresting if it is beyond sense? What colour do we want to make with this note? And how will it change as the note moves closer to the next? If we started this note with a gasp, does that mean the next needs to do the same, or can we, should we, give more or give less?

Every single note in a performance is weighed, considered, decided and rendered. But how thrilling when you feel the musicians go beyond any of that conscious music-making to the bowels of their art.

A testament to the mystery of music: in my second year at the Royal Northern College of Music, the chamber orchestra of the college went on a three-week trip to the south of France. I was the principal viola, and as you can imagine, very happy to be going there. We played concerts in Aix-en-Provence and various other small festivals around the south, and towards the end of the tour, gave a concert in a small church in a smallish village in the Alps. We were conducted by Michel Brandt, a serious, precise Frenchman who displayed his emotions only with the end of his baton. In this concert we played a Mozart Divertimento and Schubert's *Unfinished Symphony*. The tour had generally gone well, but after two weeks of travel we were getting tired and the last two concerts had been only average.

It was late afternoon, the middle of July, and a magnificent thunderstorm had threatened its way up the Alps and into the village. The doors of the church were open as we played, and I watched the light disappear as the thunderstorm came right on top of us. The pews were full of holidaymakers in shorts, old men leaning forward to hear better, and children playing in the aisles. A single woman stood in the rain, just outside the church. She let herself become soaked and didn't move throughout the concert.

The conductor, Michel, prepared to begin the Schubert. It's a tiny beginning, just the cellos and basses, very low, somehow insignificant and vengeful, a sigh of ingratitude. Beginnings like this can be tricky, as you want to be so delicate with the sound, but it still needs to project to the audience. Michel raised his baton, looked around our small orchestra to bring our attention to him, and gave one minimal movement with his right arm. When a conductor does this, they give the world of the piece with that one gesture. From the size of the movement the conductor shows the energy, from the shape of the movement they show the articulation, and from the speed of the movement they show the tempo of the piece. In the opening phrase the cellos and basses play the same notes an octave apart, which

can also be difficult, as it reveals how exact your intonation is. Or isn't. The higher octave needs to play slightly quieter than the lower, so they can sit in the protection of the lower sound. Our eyes and hearts clung to Michel's upbeat, and we entered the music. The six cellos and basses seemed bonded with an outside force. They played not as six but as one. The rain from the thunderstorm was so loud it was difficult to tell whether the audience could have heard the beginning, but when the violins entered with their shimmering accompaniment for the woodwind tune, we all felt the attention of the entire church gather. We became a congregation. The time fell away into each bar, and each bar fell away into each phrase, and each phrase fell away into the universe of the music.

Nobody knows why Schubert left this symphony unfinished. In 1822 he wrote the first two movements and started a third, a scherzo. The final movement may have been composed and used for another piece, but a common belief is that Schubert left this piece to its incomplete fate because he fell ill with syphilis around the same time. It was likely to have been the secondary stage of the disease, where the patient experiences a skin rash, often on the palms or soles of the feet, severe headaches, fever and fatigue. Schubert would probably have known the severity of his illness and that he would eventually die from it. Around this time, when Schubert was still only in his early twenties, he and a group of friends were arrested for alleged political activity. Schubert's best friend, Johann Senn, was punished and exiled from Vienna and Schubert never saw him again. It is no surprise that the music has these chasms of desolation and beams of nostalgic light.

There is a moment in the second, slower movement where the first violins are left hanging by a golden thread, suspended above the earth on a long, thin note, a high B, the home note of the whole piece but not this movement, which is an E. The suspension has happened twice already but this time it is endless as the violins slowly slip, ledge by ledge, down to an E, the home note, and then, a shock: the universe of the music makes a cosmic shift and the violins drop even further, to a C. Where have we gone? It sounds slight, but it is one of the most staggering moments in all music. You think you have arrived, and you are shoved on, ignored, as if this was never your home. It is a musical exile, with Schubert perhaps remembering and yearning for his absent friend. When you do finally reach the home note it doesn't feel like home anymore, anticipating the lack of tonal security of the Second Viennese School, with Schoenberg and Berg.

That afternoon, Michel Brandt hardly needed to conduct us. He set the tone for the performance with his presence and from there we played the Schubert as we had never played it before. We extended phrases, we pushed tempos, we leapt from the safety of our rehearsals into the arms of adventure and liberty. That afternoon, the forty members of our orchestra were a single biosystem, our ecology linked inextricably, quavers passing to quarter notes, crotchets passing to half notes, minims passing to whole notes. We depended on each other and held each other close as we travelled this unfinished universe. That afternoon everything was interconnected – music and body and instrument and mind and each other.

And at the end, when the unfinished piece finished, the woman outside stood bathed not in rain but in the light of a rainbow. All colour, all sound, vibrating as one.

It was a performance that will never be matched and will never be heard again. There were no recording machines there that afternoon, no microphones, no posterity. Only memory.

We left the stage to find Michel, a man of few words, beneath a statue of Christ and Mother Mary, a trio of weeping.

He simply said, 'It was perfect. You were all … perfect.'

Once in a while I take my viola, open my music cabinet and play through old pieces. Music is a time tunnel to a different age, not only for the world but for ourselves. Some pieces in the cabinet I first played forty years ago – Marais dances, Brahms sonatas, Bach cello suites; they have aged well and somehow look better than when we were young together. These pieces are old friends who don't mind if you haven't called them for a while, your relationship will always be bonded and unconditional.

I play these pieces now and wonder at the child who could have played them then. Technically, of course, I have improved, and my interpretation has been fed by fifty years of living, but the innocence of a twelve-year-old girl in Shropshire also knew a lot. I look at these pieces and have new respect for young me. When my young students play the same pieces, I listen closely and try to catch my youth in theirs. It never works. I look at these young players and marvel at their imagination, their perception of what can be true, their individuality. I marvel at how they change themselves from week to week so easily, with hardly a goodbye to their old self. When they have a birthday coming up, I say goodbye to their eight- or twelve-year-old self and wonder what they'll be like next week, and they laugh, shrug their shoulders and leap into their lives with no holding back, just like their music-making. These young musicians know so deeply what they are doing, they hardly know it at all.

> *We are the music makers,*
> *And we are the dreamers of dreams,*
> *Wandering by lone sea-breakers,*
> *And sitting by desolate streams; –*
> *World-losers and world-forsakers,*
> *On whom the pale moon gleams:*
> *Yet we are the movers and shakers*
> *Of the world for ever, it seems.*
>
> *With wonderful deathless ditties*
> *We build up the world's great cities,*
> *And out of a fabulous story*
> *We fashion an empire's glory:*
> *One man with a dream, at pleasure,*
> *Shall go forth and conquer a crown;*
> *And three with a new song's measure*
> *Can trample a kingdom down.*

'Ode' by Arthur O'Shaughnessy

Eric is ten years old. He is just beginning to lengthen, the last months of boyhood. A dark amazement of hair jumps into the air and Eric's large brown eyes survey the world through music. One lesson, he stops me on my way out the door.

'Ed, you know this bit?' And he plays part of a Bach minuet. 'Yes.'

'It feels really nice when I play it.'

Eric is playing Gossec's *Gavotte*, which he says also feels nice, for the end-of-year concert. It's a skipping, jumping, cartwheeling kind of piece and Eric loves it. He begins it brilliantly, but I notice that each time he plays he is getting faster and faster. He is running downhill and his legs cannot keep up. I play along with him, gently applying some cello teacher brakes to his racing wheels, until he slows up just enough, then races off again. How am I going to prove to Eric that playing a piece faster doesn't necessarily mean playing it better?

Young students often love doing things to a ridiculous exaggeration. I dare Eric to a race. We kick off the piece, playing follow the leader. Eric is very good at this, having been trained with Dr Suzuki's *Perpetual Motion* piece. I lead and push the speed to the point where Eric cannot stay with me and the music becomes senseless. I then lead Eric so, so slowly that the music becomes senseless in the other direction. Now I ask Eric to play at the speed where he feels comfortable, and where the music makes sense. He plays and the music pours from his cello as if it was there all along, he only had to open the door. The tempo has become his friend. His face is one big grin. It 'feels nice'.

'Never rush, never falter.' Advice from Dr Suzuki about progress with our music and how, if we practise steadily and regularly, we will always have firm footsteps along the path. We need never worry either about not being able to do something or being made to do something too soon.

We follow this path and realise we can. But most importantly, we realise we may.

Sometimes I have a student who has lost their magical thinking, their belief in the possibility of anything; they doubt their own playing and their ability of ever sounding or feeling as they want to with their music. They have become aware of change and doubt it and test it and are even scared of it. These students are usually in their later teen years, or adults. One student, Bradley, from my Hong Kong years, comes to mind.

When I started teaching Bradley he was already fourteen, and a skilled cellist. He loved music. You could see it in his face and body when he played – every single part of his being contributed to his sound, most of all his mind. We started lessons and I tried to persuade Bradley to change a few things, particularly his bow hold. Bow holds can become tense and imbalanced if they are not tended to, and Bradley's was out of kilter. He started to change and his playing began to improve, but after a few months I noticed there was something holding Bradley down to the ground: he was scared of making a beautiful sound. I know this because every time Bradley did make a beautiful, rich, sonorous sound, his body flinched and drew into itself, his back slouched and he stopped playing, often mid-piece. He would go over the same phrase note for note, stopping and repeating, until it became impossible to know where he was in the music. 'Just play, Bradley, just let it flow!' I would say, not yet knowing Peter Luff's wittier 'you need to get the car started to tune the engine'. But Bradley's beautiful sound would stop him every time. What could I do? I knew music meant so much to him, but every time he came close, he ran away. And then I realised. Bradley didn't want to change. He was holding on to his old pieces, his old sound, his old technique, because that is what he had always known. He didn't want to say goodbye. I just had to wait and trust that, in the end, Bradley would forget his old sound and embrace his new. He did, but it took about two years. Both of us nearly lost hope, several times, but we came through it, him a much better cellist, me a much better teacher. Sometimes we just need to forget.

———————————————

There is a look I see in my students' faces, and in their bodies, when they forget what they cannot do and realise what they can.

Mia is an eleven-year-old student who swapped from violin to viola a couple of years ago. She loves to do gymnastics when she comes for her viola lesson, and her intellect and wit are as flashy as her cartwheels. One of the great advances in recent years is the availability and quality of smaller musical instruments, so even though Mia is young, she could start playing on a very small viola, and as she grows, her viola can grow with her. When I first started learning viola I played on a violin strung as a viola, which sounded terrible and was the equivalent of a small child wearing their parents' clothes: they might be wearing them in the right places, but the clothes are disguising the true size of the child. Now there's a size to fit every few months of growth.

Mia takes her instrument from its case and we warm up and play a revision piece, work a little bit on her new piece, then we play her polished piece. This is a classic Suzuki method way of teaching where the student always has something old, something new and something easily within their range of ability. They are being stretched and confirmed simultaneously.

Some students don't like the pieces in the Suzuki method, and if they don't like the music, it's very simple: they will not practise the music. I have learnt over the years to be much more flexible about repertoire, and I go off into different books to find out what they do like and will therefore play. Mia is a big fan of romantic ballads, so I write out some big hits like Josh Groban's *You Raise Me Up*, Coldplay's *Fix You* and the theme from *Titanic*, with Leonardo flying from the bow of the ship, for Mia to play. Changing the music means everything to her. The music is not foreign to Mia anymore, and now she delights in making it her own.

Mia takes her viola and swings it up under her chin, a pro in the making. She takes her bow with a determined hold, finds the perfect place for her first note and starts playing. It's such a difference from before, when we were playing music Mia didn't care about as much. Then she only did the minimum necessary to move on, but now, as her bow glides smoothly over the strings of her viola, the bow of the *Titanic* stands defiant above the Atlantic Ocean. As Mia goes through the waves of the music, she stands tall and proud beside Leonardo DiCaprio, both lost in the moment, both perceptive to where they have come from, where they might go, and delighting in where they are. Mia's music is her pride, her enthusiasm, her power, her gift to the world.

Mia's music is the way she feels about herself.

F:
HOPE

To send light into the
darkness of men's hearts –
such is the duty of the artist.

ROBERT SCHUMANN

———————————

SATURDAY MORNINGS ARE THE SAME all around the country for music teachers. In Brisbane, a cascade of children tumble into my teaching room, one at a time, ready for music.

Each child's entry is unique: some burst through the door, forgetting how wide their cello case is and get stuck, some amble in with all the insouciance of a seasoned pro, some romp in with their brothers, puppies mid-fight. But my favourites are the cartwheelers.

They put their cases down first (phew), throw their hands up in the air, raise a leg and hurl themselves into the most glorious spins and twirls all around the room. I've tried to emulate them, with only polite approval and some comment that my legs aren't quite straight. Hmm, children. Tough critics.

They eventually settle down and open their cases while we chat about their week. As their little hands prepare their instruments, they bring tales of sport and siblings and books and who has done what in their class and how strict their teacher is and how they were naughty and their dad had to tell them off and how they superglued their doll to the dining room table and their mum had to spend the evening picking it off but mum didn't mind too much because she was drinking a really big glass of wine.

Artie enters, his feet beginning to turn out from his ballet training, his face a souvenir of chocolate milk. Artie is nine years old and a gloriously rambunctious cellist. He's the one who is a Yo-Yo Ma in the making. Recently, Artie has been learning to play with his left hand in new places on the fingerboard (shifting) and exploring some Bach minuets, and we have also been polishing the Robert Schumann song *The Happy Farmer* for the end-of-year concert. Artie dives into his playing and can sometimes race through a piece terrifyingly fast. With *The Happy Farmer*, he plays so fast I imagine some accelerating modern technology has come to the agricultural world, rather than a ruddy farmer with a pitchfork. This is a tricky piece, with lots of complex bow directions and string crossings, and if you play it too quickly it's very easy to fall over. Artie is nimble and skips through it, the ruddy farmer left for dust, then surprises me with a piece we haven't learnt yet. Artie's older brother Bill is a bold, charismatic cellist and a while ago played a song called *The Two Grenadiers* by Schumann. It's a grim tale of two French soldiers in the Napoleonic wars who are captured in Russia, released, find out they lost the war and Napoleon has been captured, and express their love for each other and their country by singing the Marseillaise at the end. Oh, and I think at least one of them dies. The music is full of high drama, made better by a child's imagination, and Artie has caught this piece in his head and he won't let it go. In one of his lessons he just starts playing it, with no input from me. Artie captures the terror and the despair of the two soldiers as they realise everything is lost, then the defiance as they sing the Marseillaise, and okay, maybe a few technical things need some more work, but the spirit, the music is there. It's not just there, it is flooding out of Artie until he cannot hold it back. He doesn't want to hold it back. Artie expresses perfectly what every musician wants to say: he loves music. He loves it for its passion, its variety, its joy, its humour, its ambiguity, its humanity, its drama, its challenge, its beauty. Artie shows why we play, and how simple the desire can be. He doesn't get lost in the reverence and awe of certain pieces or composers, he isn't scared by a new technical challenge or sound, he just grabs his cello, throws his limbs around it and plays the heart out of it. I learn a lot from Artie.

Artie surprised me with *The Two Grenadiers*, but there are other students who have the same obsession with a piece of music. Many of my adult students come to me with a dream of a piece they want to play, and they slowly, slowly, year by year, come closer to that piece. And then they play it.

I have been teaching Cathy for three years, and she is developing very well. Cathy started lessons in her late forties and gave herself three years to see if she could get anywhere. She's about to go into her fourth year, so I'm guessing she's as happy with her progress as I am. Cathy has a busy family life and a very demanding full-time job, but she makes time every day to do her cello practice. In the first year, as is so often the case with adults, she raced through Suzuki cello book one, then the second, faced the many challenges of the third and is about to begin some solo Bach. At the end of last year, Cathy left the room where we were having our lesson and came back with some sheet music in her hand, a beautiful Bärenreiter edition of the viola da gamba sonatas by J.S. Bach.

'Ed, do you think, some day, I might be able to play this?'

Years ago, Cathy went to see the film *Truly, Madly, Deeply* with her sister. It's a film about a cellist, played by Alan Rickman, who dies and leaves behind his grieving wife, a pianist, played by Juliet Stevenson. It's a story of the journey through loss and grief and acceptance, and the film is also suffused with the most glorious music. As Cathy says, 'It just hit me. My sister and I came out of the cinema and both of us said, wouldn't it be wonderful to be able to play the cello, and to play that!'

The music Cathy fell in love with is Bach's slow movement from the third sonata for viola da gamba (or cello) and keyboard in G minor.

The viola da gamba is from the Renaissance family of viols, similar to the violin family, but, as a forest is slowly consumed by a real estate developer, the viols were overtaken by the violin family for a slightly depressing reason: violins, violas and cellos were louder and more suitable for virtuosic solo playing. This sonata, one of the last written for viola da gamba, is now often played on the cello or the viola, which I feel is rubbing the dear viola da gamba players' noses in it. Still, no matter which instrument it is played by, this music is bewitching and cosmic. The slow movement begins with a whole note on the cello, held up by soft pacing on the keyboard below, the cello note going on, and on, and on, over the horizon, until we are led into a garden of sonic delights. And once we are there, we are taken along paths of reconciliation, grace and elegance. In the middle of the movement, the music brings us to a questioning: is this real? Is life really this perfect, in all its imperfection? And the music tells us, yes and yes and yes, and each note gets better, and better. This is heaven made human. The earthly ingredients of the instrument – animal gut, horsehair, tree resin, maple and pine – are lifted higher than the stars and deeper than the tree roots. With its complete abstraction, this piece inspires reverence and awe. It is, quite simply, music beyond pain.

Cathy, who was about thirty at this point, bought the sheet music for the sonata and played that at home on the piano, but the idea of playing the cello became sidetracked by life – travel, marriage, two children – and when I met Cathy she had reached her late forties.

We talk about the moment Cathy decided to start cello lessons.

'When my girls started learning music, I was watching them get enjoyment out of learning an instrument and I felt really jealous! I thought, I don't have an instrument, my husband plays guitar, so everyone else had an instrument but I didn't. Then Georgie [Cathy's daughter] started having lessons with you, and I thought, I'll just ask.' She smiles. 'But I thought I was too old. It was a foolish endeavour. I thought cello was not the sort of thing you started as an adult. If I'd had a piano I could have quite comfortably picked up piano lessons again, but to start an instrument from ground zero …'

So what does Cathy think now? Does she still think it was a foolish endeavour?

'I'm so glad I did it. But it's hard as an adult to be really rubbish at it at the beginning. It's where you need to start, but it's deeply uncomfortable. Playing the cello has taught me patience. Watching my daughter learn has reminded me how similar we are – we both make faces when we make a mistake, we are in a hurry to "get there".' Cathy laughs. 'The cello is the canary in the coalmine – the last few years have been very stressful for me, so playing the cello tells me when I'm stressed, as then I can't make a good sound; it forces me to stop and be in the moment and concentrate on that. I can use music as a salve.'

What would Cathy say to her thirty-year-old self, when she first dreamt of playing the cello?

'Fifteen or so years when I didn't play any music at all and I could have been playing music, it seems absurd to me now that I didn't just do it then. And I would have felt less foolish starting it then, as a thirty-year-old. But that was a time in my life when I was spending all my money on travel. I would have thought, that's a plane ticket.'

And now, after learning the cello for three years, Cathy is playing Handel and Lully and Dvořák, and, probably at the end of this year, she will be starting to learn the Bach sonata she first heard all those years ago. The satisfaction of achieving her dream is beyond words.

'It's important to feel the joy and remember why you got into it in the first place. I love it. Now I can't imagine not doing it.'

––––––––––

The joys of music for my mother were few and far between. My memories of childhood are of my mother alone in her challenges, hard work and very occasional happiness, no-one to really speak to except her family, and us too close and too distant to communicate. Loneliness must be the worst thing to happen to any of us. Witnessing her loneliness was a lesson for me in the power of that experience, and that we all will go through it someday. But if you can survive it, you can survive anything. And playing music teaches us to be satisfied in our loneliness, because for any musician, reaching the level where you can audition for music college – and are accepted – means you have almost certainly spent an epoch of time on your own.

From early childhood, where you might be playing your instrument with the supervision of a parent every day for thirty minutes, to teenage years, when you start to explore what you want in your life and commit to two or three hours of practice, by the time you reach eighteen you will have spent approximately seven thousand hours on your own. Seven thousand hours devoted to developing sound production, co-ordination, memory, concentration, intonation, musical style and historical knowledge, finger agility, speed and strength, musical phrasing, articulation and the creation of truth in beauty.

Sure, musicians play with other people and have lessons, but the real work is done on your own. Just you and your instrument.

You get up early to squeeze in your practice before school. If you're at college, you get up even earlier to claim a room before anyone else does, and these places are no musical Garden of Eden. Practice rooms are often very, very small with no windows, and the combined sounds of other musicians through the walls comes to you like a distant musical battle.

But musicians are never on their own. All those facets of practice become like friends (or maybe frenemies sometimes) to the musician. We develop a superhuman inner ear, imagination and inner life. We live inside music. We take the terror of loneliness, and, with our musical alchemy, turn it into a solace. To be alone is to be able to create art for others. So when we are saturated by loneliness, not those obvious times when a parent or partner dies or we are moving towns or schools, but when perhaps we have missed ourselves, only music can get in and give us hope.

————————————

These five years since I came to Brisbane from Kabul have mirrored another type of journey, and one I only see now in hindsight: a journey of bereavement. For a long time I thought transitioning would be entirely joyful, perhaps with a few bumps along the way of hormones and surgeries and some social difficulties, but I understand now it is a pilgrimage not only through joy but also grief.

The original grief of shock, and refusing to accept who I was, all those years ago when I was cycling in Pakistan.

The grief of being transgender in a cis-centred world, and my guilt at what I would do to my family. This must be my fault, so I am not allowed to do anything about it.

The grief of being consumed by anger. Why me? Why not my siblings? What did my parents do? Why do I have to endure this endless battle of hormones? Surely if I just ignore it, it will go away. Won't it?

The grief at what I will need to go through. What will I lose? Who will I lose?

The grief of what might have been, and my childhood, my 'real' childhood, never lived.

A surrendering of grief, because it simply cannot continue. I must find a way. I need to act.

And finally, the achievement that this grief does not define me. I am more than a transgender man. I will transition, it will be hard, but it will be glorious. I will go through one of life's many great challenges and I will share my story, so that people might understand. I will let my past die, and I will let it be reborn in the new me. From Emma to Ed. A transformation from grief to hope.

Just like learning an instrument, the tribulations, the perplexities of transitioning do fade away. Well, except the girls, my ovaries, who are still kicking – five years now of being carpet-bombed with testosterone and they are still pumping out that oestrogen. Within my abdomen, I still occasionally have my own battle of the sexes; it is not pretty, it is often very uncomfortable, and at the moment my money is on oestrogen winning. I feel I should one day donate the girls to science for posterity. Girls aside, I can go weeks now without even thinking about being transgender, just as I can go weeks playing my viola without thinking about a technical challenge. (I know, that's an open goal for a viola joke.) Even on the horn, if I am playing a simple piece, I can just think of the music, not worry about the inside. I think of the song, not the sorrow.

As the sadness sinks, the joys surface. I am learning the poetry and cadence and ease and the brotherhood of men. I am learning the subtlety of male communication, both physical and spoken. I am learning that the slightest of nods as you pass a man is equivalent in my old world to a lengthy hug. I am learning that when a man calls you 'buddy', it is the sweetest feeling imaginable. I am learning to wait in a conversation, just like a viola part in a symphony. I am learning that men will leave many rests in the sound, many silences, and that men's speech may often be of few words, but those words have a chord of meanings below them.

One night at dinner with my friends Brenton and Miranda, I knew I was really changing.

I used to play in a quartet with Brenton and Miranda and their son, Martin. Every time I go to Melbourne we meet up for dinner and play through some Mozart or Haydn afterwards. We could play before dinner, but after a bottle of Rutherglen shiraz we always seem to sound so much better. Anyway, a couple of years into my transition I was there with Charlie, and that evening I noticed something. You remember from before, when I had been left with a group of men standing in a circle and all they could talk about was cars? This evening, at one point I noticed that Charlie was speaking with Miranda about one of her students in what sounded like an intense and fascinating conversation, and I was chatting with Martin and Brenton about … you guessed it. Cars. And I couldn't have been happier.

It is coming close to the end of the year and Rosie is preparing for her performance in my student concert. I am most keen to hear what she is going to wear, as I know she is the owner of a blue tutu and I feel this would be a glorious addition to any concert.

'No, I'm going to wear my green dress!' Rosie is adamant, despite some undignified pleading from my part, so to distract myself we go through her old pieces and decide which one to perform.

The choice of which piece to perform is crucial. Especially for Rosie's first public performance. I have seen people perform pieces where they are more killing the music than playing it; Rosie needs to love her piece, but it also needs to sit comfortably within her technical capability.

Rosie already has abundant self-knowledge, so I ask her which piece she thinks will work best. I have a feeling we will choose the same piece.

'Hmm. Well, I really like *Go Tell Aunt Rhody*, but I've only just started that. And I really like *Stew Pot Hop*, but that's really easy now so that would be boring to play. I know – this one!'

And with her fast cello fingers, Rosie points at the exact song I wanted her to point at: *French Folk Song*.

French Folk Song is an anthem for cello students around the world. It is similar to *Ode to Joy*: the same key, D major, and essentially a scale going up and down and around. It sits so comfortably in your body that, even though I have played it twelve million times, I still love it. It gives you a chance to create a beautiful bell sound and to explore where the bow sits best on the string, and it's a piece we return to as we improve with our playing. We can play it with different home notes, and eventually play it very high on the cello at the far end of the fingerboard. *French Folk Song* is our font of wisdom.

I want Rosie to play from memory at the concert, but we both need to make sure she is ready. Being able to play a piece in a lesson is very different from playing it with the added stress of strangers staring at you, so we begin concert practice.

First, we just play it through and enjoy it. I play harmony with Rosie, and we talk about the mood of each phrase, and the physicality of how it feels. Stepping up with some fingers, hopping off with others, changing strings on a push or a pull, the waterfall of notes at the end. Then we play a phrase each. If Rosie can follow the music mentally while I'm playing, then come in with the next phrase, this shows she is holding the music well in her mind. We play it at different speeds, dynamics, and then, as Rosie is getting tired, I purposely ask her to do some jumping jacks to elevate her heart rate and she plays it again.

This is interspersed with learning her new piece, *May Song*, and in the next lesson I set the alarm for every ten minutes at which point we play *French Folk Song* without warming up, no matter what else we might be doing. It is working. Rosie is playing the piece with hardly a conscious thought, and the music is beginning to shine. Rosie is doing what professional musicians do: practising until they can't get it wrong. Rosie says she's a bit nervous for the concert, but I can see, underneath her words, she is also aware of how well she is playing. Rosie plays her cello, adjusts her finger position, her bow position, her bow speed and her intention, and with each note she is asking, 'How can it get any better than this?'

And with each note, the music is showing her how.

––––––––––––

Peter Luff plays the opening of Strauss's *Ein Heldenleben* (*A Hero's Life*) and I want to listen to the horn forever. And I wonder, will I ever be able to play just a little like that? Up close, a superb horn player like Peter has a completely different sound from in the concert hall or a recording. You now know many of the challenges of playing the horn, but there's another: when you are playing in an orchestra your sound is pointing backwards. If you think of trumpets or trombones, their bells point to the front of the hall, but the horns point to the back. This means a horn player must anticipate the music and play slightly before everyone else, as their sound needs to go backwards and bounce

234

off the rear stage wall to come forwards again. The great British conductor and wit Sir Thomas Beecham summed it up when he asked the concertmaster of the orchestra to tell the horns they were playing late.

'But Sir Thomas,' he said, 'they haven't arrived at the rehearsal yet.'

'Tell them anyway. It will save time later.'

Because the horn's sound must travel much further than other instruments, it needs extra thrust and texture in its momentum. Peter told me about the great Australian horn player Barry Tuckwell. When you listened to Tuckwell's sound up close, it was richly complex, but out in the auditorium it was perhaps the smoothest sound to ever come from the horn. Horn players must perfectly assess how pre-emptive and how abrasive they must be, to appear completely smooth and in time. A horn player must play in the here and now but have a projection of their sound over there and into the future.

I have been making some headway with my exam pieces – Euridice now only dies three times each play-through – and Peter has given me a concert piece to perform at some point. I'm hoping that the 'some point' does not arrive too soon, like that unexpected D arriving the other day when I was trying to play a C. Ho hum. My new concert piece (how cool does that sound?) is Saint-Saëns' *Romance* in F major. This music was written for French horn player Jean-Henri Garigue, and back in the late nineteenth century would have been played on the hand horn – no valves, no switching between shorter or longer piping, just the horn player, their embouchure, their diaphragm, and their hand shape in the bell. Changing your hand shape in the bell is lesson three hundred and twenty-seven in horn playing, and since I'm only at lesson fifteen, Peter is encouraging the use of my valves. I am too. And so are my neighbours. Although I do have a go at the beginning just playing with the harmonic series on the open horn and it's surprisingly successful. When I listen to recordings of the romance, particularly by the historical horn specialist Anneke Scott, the open hand horn brings a visceral reality to the sound, a sound of nature rather than dreams. You can hear the muscle of the music.

I start the piece in my next lesson, and once again Peter gives me one of his gems.

'Imagine the start of this note sounding like a marshmallow dropped onto a feather pillow.'

Oh my gosh. I want to immediately go to a marshmallow and feather pillow shop, buy some marshmallows and a feather pillow (rather than the slightly lumpy one I currently have) and drop marshmallows onto said pillow all afternoon. Then I can say I've done my horn practice. As that drops in my mind I begin the piece again and my first note sounds like a bag of nails crashing onto a steel girder. Oh dear.

Romance has one of my dreaded high Gs, just a short one, and as I play through the piece for Peter, I reach this spot, and because I now have a 'thing' about high Gs, of course I cannot do anything else but splutter and crash. I notice that even when I see one coming in the distance, my process of breathing, embouchure and sound begins to fail, a coward in the face of struggle. But then I realise that it is not a struggle. It does not need to be a struggle. If I can only take my ego away and think about the process and the music, the G will slot in where it needs to, naturally. As I follow Peter's guidance to blow beyond the horn, to allow my lips to open like a bud into the mouthpiece, I approach the G from an F and it releases itself, just another note, with still a way to go in smoothness of tone, but it's a start. And when you can do something once, that means it is inside you to do again, and again.

Peter wisdoms (new verb), 'There you are! Follow the process, and you are bound to be successful. You just need one note, one note ...'

And the best thing is, now that I know I can do it, the next time will be less concerning, and so I have just stepped into a virtuous circle. But since it's the horn, the next time I play the passage I crash catastrophically off the G. That circle is looking a little skew-whiff to me.

At the end of the lesson, Peter shocks me by asking if I would like to come and play with his horn class at the Queensland Conservatorium. Bear in mind, Peter's tertiary students are among the best young horn players in the country, and many of Peter's students go on to play in orchestras internationally. It is the horn equivalent of me being asked to train with the Australian Olympic swim team.

'Really? But ... will I be able to ... ?' I want to say 'survive', but instead I come out with the feeble 'manage'.

'You'll be fine – just do what you can. See you next Wednesday at 9 a.m. at the Nepalese Peace Pagoda.'

The pagoda was handcrafted by one hundred and sixty Nepalese families in Kathmandu over two years, assembled at the 1988 Brisbane Expo, then purchased for the city through donations. It sits next to the Brisbane River, and, conveniently for Peter's horn class, right outside the Brisbane Conservatorium.

I arrive the following Wednesday at 8.17 a.m. (I hate being late). But now I have time to glean some calm from the Buddhist statues before Peter's class. The students arrive en masse on the dot of nine, walking in formation, horns in hand, a crack squad of music cadets. I want to cry and run away, but Peter introduces me and we head into our hour of elite horn warmups.

A memory of my swimming lesson with Helentherese surfaces. I have just taken off my flotation aids and am now being asked to swim five kilometres. At pace. With racing turns.

We dive in. The beginning isn't so bad. We start off with elevators, and even though these young people are taking their elevators up to the twelfth floor and beyond when I am only going to the eighth, I can still keep my head above water. But it stops there. I start slowly but most leadenly to sink. Peter then leads his troops through an extraordinary series of musical acrobatics that include scales, long notes, long low notes, long high notes, low notes leaping impossibly to high notes, high notes leaping foolhardily to low notes, arpeggios hopping through the notes in between and the players doing something with their embouchures that I still don't quite understand. All the while I play where I can and am helped along by a master's student, Ben, who is very kind, shows me which note they're playing, and gives lovely advice like 'use lots of air'. And then, at the end of this masterclass in youthful genius, horn roulette. This is a brutal challenge where Peter starts on a C and the students go around in a circle, rising a semitone each time. If you crack the note, you're out. Fine, I figure. I should be able to last a round. The roulette reaches me and all I need to play is an easy E, and guess what? I stuff it up. I am out first go.

Did I say an 'easy E'? Nothing, nothing, is easy on the horn.

At the end the students come over and congratulate me on how far I've come, but all I want to do is call the national papers and TV stations and say, look at these young people! Our country spends so much money and effort and time and attention on sportspeople, and these young musicians are achieving easily as much, work just as hard, and yet remain uncelebrated and unsupported by proper funding and attention. These are our stars, as well as our sportspeople, and their artistry and craft give as much to our society as any person doing fancy things with a funny-shaped ball. These young people are doing even fancier things with a funny-shaped instrument.

It's been five years since my return from Kabul, and over these years, work came slowly, but it did come. After all that soaking anxiety when I first thought of transitioning that I would have no work, no family, no friends, nothing, it turned out I couldn't have been more wrong. In 2017 I presented a weekly art show on Radio National (art on the radio is surprisingly visual), and in the middle of 2018 I received a call from ABC Classic: the weekend breakfast presenter, Christopher Lawrence, had decided to leave and they wondered if I would like to return. I have never felt so welcomed as I was by the ABC Classic audience. It was a homecoming.

My teaching studio grew steadily over those years too. Student numbers were eventually large enough that I could resign from the school where they told me which toilet I should use, and I could stay closer to home. An opening also came up at a nearby state school to give strings lessons as a private teacher, so I applied and went for an interview. I sat with the principal and the head of resources, and at the end, when they offered me the job, I thought it only polite to tell them I am transgender, as there was going to be some press about me.

'Well, does it make any difference to how you teach?' the principal, Michael, asked.

'No, absolutely not.'

'Well, then, it doesn't make any difference to us.'

And that was that. I'm still teaching there.

—————————————

I'm sitting in the music room at the school with Daniel. He is twelve years old and has been studying cello with me for about three years. He practises thoroughly and regularly so has made impressive progress. He is playing throughout the range of the cello from first position to thumb position, plays with a variety of colours and articulations, has excellent intonation and, most important of all, has a curiosity to find out how his playing can sound even richer.

Daniel and I have been working on a piece by Tchaikovsky – his *Chanson Triste*, or *Sad Song* – for the end-of-year concert, and Daniel has been searching for the perfect line.

Musicians are endlessly searching for the perfect line, the perfect progression, the perfect decision, the perfect beginning, the perfect ending. And when we achieve this, our music flows from us with ease, joy and glory.

Tchaikovsky composed his *Chanson Triste* as part of a group of piano pieces called *12 Pieces of Moderate Difficulty*. If only all life could be so clearly titled.

Buying a house in an Australian capital city? *A Purchase of Impossible Difficulty.*

Making a croquembouche? *A Trial of Achievable Difficulty.*

Playing the horn? How much *Difficulty* can you manage?

Perhaps Tchaikovsky was feeling in a pedantic mood when he gave these pieces their title. He was certainly going through a terrible time in his life: his marriage to Antonina, one of his students, had lasted two and a half months and Tchaikovsky was persuading Antonina to apply for divorce. It is only now being recognised in Russia that Tchaikovsky was homosexual; this marriage was an attempt to stem rumours about his private life in a country where to be homosexual was, is, a risk to yourself and your family. Tchaikovsky had thought Antonina was unintelligent and malleable enough to provide what he wanted, which was essentially a celibate marriage and for Tchaikovsky to continue to have sex with men. Yes, that's right, Tchaikovsky wanted everything. When Antonina did exactly the opposite – i.e., was not malleable and did want sex – it drove Tchaikovsky into such mental distress that his brother took him on an extended tour of Western Europe, then to their sister's estate in Ukraine, where he composed *Chanson Triste*. Despite Tchaikovsky's efforts, he and Antonina never divorced, and Antonina spent the final two decades of her life in a mental hospital. So not only is this music a sad song, most of Antonina's life was a sad song.

Talking about all this with a twelve-year-old is hardly age-appropriate, so Daniel and I discuss what might be mildly sad in his own life, to get in the right mood. Quite a lot, as it turns out. Particularly the flavour he wanted having sold out at the ice-cream shop and him crashing his bicycle at the bottom of a treacherous hill. As Daniel starts to play, a certain mood descends around him, a mood from beyond his own existence, a mood that reaches out to the ether and pulls in the sound of Tchaikovsky. Daniel has stepped into the river of music. From the very first note, a cello version of a marshmallow dropping on a pillow, Daniel pulls us in to the sorrow and solitude of Tchaikovsky as he tried in so many terrible ways to fit in with society. The song is a lament to denying your true self, and it portrays the cost. Daniel seems to understand this and gathers a sense of despair that no young person should know. Daniel is a true musician because he imagines not only what is but what might be. Daniel has found the perfect line.

That line is always there, whether we are just beginning or have been playing music for years. Whether we are playing an instrument or listening to recordings, there is a moment where our self is bonded to the music and nothing else matters. Our existence reveals itself in its purest form, as vibration, and all notes become one. When we find that line, we feel, in our deepest place, a reconciliation of self, a bringing together of the front and back, and a recognition that playing music is a gift to ourselves at an unfathomable level.

———————————

In the words of Benjamin Anderson, bass trombonist with Orchestra Victoria in Melbourne, 'I think one of the interesting things I've noticed, for both me and for a lot of musicians, is how profound the loss has been over this year. It became really hard to actually engage in listening to music; it was triggering to listen to, because it reminded you of your personal loss.'

Benjamin, along with many musicians around the world, spent much of 2020 in musical silence. From the last performance before the midyear lockdown in Melbourne to the next performance, Benjamin had two hundred and fifty days where he could only play on his own, at home. How does a musician cope with this? And what happens to them when they do play in a group again?

His role as bass trombonist in the orchestra is unique. You may ask what a bass trombone does in an orchestra – isn't a trombone and a tuba enough? As Benjamin puts it, like goalkeepers in football, you only notice bass trombones when they're terrible. As opposed to violas, which he says you only notice when they're excellent. The bass trombone has a crucial role as the glue between the low end of the orchestra – tuba, double bass, bassoon, low clarinets, timpani – and the high end. So, despite Benjamin being a little judgey about the violas, the roles of viola and bass trombone are remarkably similar.

'The orchestra is kind of this miraculous organism. Everyone is focused on their individual skill and refinement of their craft to create something that is no longer about the individual.' As Benjamin says, to play successfully in an orchestra, in any ensemble, you need to let go of your ego and yet be a complete authority on your instrument.

Every time a musician takes their instrument or voice in their hands and practises, it is a step into hope. But it isn't an empty hope, it is an active one, because they are doing something to improve themselves, and generally, there is a reason to practise – a concert or an audition. When the lockdown in Melbourne happened, Benjamin needed to hold on to hope that concerts would start again but also needed to remain pragmatic when there was essentially nothing to practise for. He couldn't look too far ahead, but he needed to maintain a relationship with his trombone so that when the concerts did restart, he was ready.

'For me it comes down simply to touch. What we're doing is such fine motor control, I need to be in touch with how things are going to work and how things are going to respond. Brass playing is a confidence game, so when you go to articulate a note, you have absolute confidence in the embouchure, the air speed, the tongue placement that it's just going to do what you want, so that all you're focusing on is the music. To get that, for me, involves a lot of routine-based exercises that put me in touch with knowing how I get from one part of the instrument to another across the whole range, across the dynamic spectrum, with different types of articulation.'

As my own beginner's journey into horn playing has taught me, playing a brass instrument has unique inner challenges. Benjamin describes the aims of his practice. 'Can I pick up my instrument and play the note of my choosing, right when I want to? That, on a brass instrument, is not a given. You have to be able to hear the note in your head and know in your system, physically, what it feels like, to imagine what it feels like before you do it. There's a kind of meditative part to keeping in touch with your instrument. Very fine changes can have a very dramatic effect, so it's about doing slow, easy exercises that remind me what needs to happen physically. Feeling it, finding it, from a place of kinaesthetic memory. Doing that every day.

'When you think about the level of fine motor control that's going on, it's extraordinary. It's a couple of millimetres in the embouchure between a wide range of notes; we calibrate our air speed to know physically that this level of air speed and this level of lip tension will produce a note in this range with this dynamic. It's kind of a ridiculous feat to expect from a body.'

As he has since he was a boy, Benjamin practised, and practised, and practised. For two hundred and fifty days. He practised for two hours a day, at least, so that when the day did come and he could play with his colleagues again, he was ready. The day did finally come, but Benjamin says the transformation of space was hard, from a small room in his flat to a concert hall. There were also other challenges that were impossible to prepare for at home.

Musicians playing together must not only play their own parts perfectly in tune, with excellent rhythm, sound, dynamics and articulation, they must also blend with the other hundred or so people in the orchestra so that they sound as one, not as one hundred. But this can only be practised when you're together, not when you're in individual lockdowns. When Orchestra Victoria started rehearsing once more, Benjamin noticed the little anxieties creep up on him.

'All the insecurities you have as a musician around "am I in tune, am I blending, am I placing my notes the same as everyone else", all of that was heightened, because that muscle memory of what rehearsals are like wasn't there. All of what I was saying about brass being a confidence game comes into play, because now you're questioning and second-guessing decisions, rather than going, "Right, I know this note is here" … As soon as a few people have questions then all those questions and doubts magnify. One of the hardest things about coming back was not having that self-confidence.'

But it is all so worth it. Benjamin says the absence of music has allowed him to comprehend even more the glories of playing in an orchestra.

'It is something quite extraordinary, thinking of the individual things I go through to refine my craft, and that there's anywhere between fifty and one hundred other people doing the same thing, and we come together as an ensemble and create something that has a unified whole. It's mind-boggling. Whether you're interested in orchestral music or not, the idea of that as an accomplishment, purely to create something of beauty and meaning, and for no other reason, there's a really special and important place for that in any society.'

Why do musicians practise? Why do musicians play? Why do we sit in a room, alone and unknown, and listen again and again to sounds from beyond the centuries and the lands where we live? As we look inside our listening and our playing, as we look inside our sound, is it in the hope we may find a way to express what we didn't even know we felt? Is our collective receiving and offering of music a manifestation of us looking towards the harbour, and our song the way to reach the shore? Is the perfecting of our individual voice our contribution and hope for the perfection of the whole?

And is the silencing of music the losing sight of our goal? I'm reminded of *Grey Funnel Line* by Cyril Tawney. The singer, a sailor in the Royal Navy, tells of the hardest time at sea being when the sun goes down, that devastating moment when they can no longer see where they are headed. And the constant desire to return home:

> Oh Lord, if dreams were only real,
> Then I'd feel my hands on that wooden wheel.
> And with all my heart I'd turn her 'round
> And tell the boys that we're homeward bound.

Our songs pull us in to shore. Each from different points, each at different speeds, each with different pauses along the way. We listen to each other, we help each other, we wait for each other, but we must stay on our own path and we must play our own part. We must follow our own inner compass. But we all are aiming for the same place – our true selves.

G:
LOVE

Let it go,
Let it out,
Let it all unravel,
Let it free
And it will be
A path on which to travel.

MICHAEL LEUNIG

IT WAS TIME to have my breasts cut off.

There is an anxiety, a yawning fear before starting gender transition, that voice, that weak internal commentator who says over and over again: 'What if you're wrong? What if you're wrong? You're an idiot – why do you think you're transgender? This isn't going to solve your problems, you know. You'll only end up some in-between weirdo and people will feel sorry for you.' Despite the enormous fear, you must trust that all those fucking years during which you now wished you had done something about it, all that desperate time, was a good thing, because now you *know*, you know like you've never known anything as completely before.

I came back from Kabul to Brisbane for my operation with Dr Alys Saylor, a plastic surgeon specialising in breast enhancement, reduction, reconstruction after cancer treatment and transgender reshaping. For me this would involve an incision on both sides, the nipples removed, the breast tissue removed, the skin sewn tight again and the nipples replaced with internal, invisible stitching in the more masculine position (less in the middle, more on the side – you can check your own). Dr Saylor is a gift to transgender men in Australia. Not only is her work flawless, she does it with huge compassion and directness. I had heard horror stories of transgender men essentially being butchered by surgeons abroad, their chests an unimaginable horror of scar and displaced nipples. Transitioning is hard enough without a botched surgery to deal with, although many transgender people do. It's heartbreaking. From Kabul I had had a phone consultation with Dr Saylor, but I needed to go in and see her in person as soon as I returned to Brisbane. It was a week before my operation.

I sat on the rear deck of the ferry, curling down the graces of the Brisbane River. The metaphor of riding a current was not lost on me. I had come from the deserts of Afghanistan, where the ground shook with bombs, to the waters of Queensland, where I was lulled into peace. It was hot, and I thought how in a few weeks I could sit with no bra and undo my shirt to feel the wind rush over my whole chest, how I could sit free and unencumbered by those limited signs of womanhood. I had breasts but I was no woman, and I knew women who had no breasts. I sat soaking in the mustard Brisbane sun and listened to Morten Lauridsen's *O Magnum Mysterium*, a setting of the fourth responsorial for Christmas Day.

O Magnum Mysterium,

et admirabile sacramentum,

ut animalia viderent Dominum natum,

iacentem in praesepio!

Beata Virgo, cujus viscera

meruerunt portare

Dominum Iesum Christum.

Alleluia!

O great mystery,

and wonderful sacrament,

that animals should see the newborn Lord,

lying in a manger!

Blessed is the Virgin, whose womb

was worthy to bear

Christ the Lord.

Alleluia!

No matter how deep, how complete the desire to change, there is still a part that resists, that denies, up to the very last minute. How could you possibly change yourself to become happy? Who gave you that right? My mind was a collision of identity. Who was I? And did I love myself enough to accept my true self, to accept what I needed to do? On that ferry ride, as the choir of Voces8 sang the Lauridsen, the doubting internal commentator finally surrendered.

Was it the words? The idea of new life being born in innocence and shared for all the world to see? The idea of a mystery being within us all, we only need take the time and contemplation to see what lies within ourselves? The idea of a divine grace being available to us all, no matter how lowly, how poor, how simple? The idea that a profound reality is there, we need only open our hearts?

Or was it the opening chord, one built not on the home note of the piece, a D, but instead on the next note of the home chord, an F sharp? Already Lauridsen has lifted us off the ground, and in that chord has added another lift, an inner step to the second of the scale, hidden a little in the tenor line. In that first bar, Lauridsen gives us the first five notes of the scale, but he does it in such a subtle, kind way, they meld into your heart with no fuss, no resistance. It is atonal, it is tonal, it is black, it is white, it is simple, it contains the world. That first phrase pulls my mind into silence and my heart into action. And as the phrases walk on, the chords lift higher off the ground, the basses never touching the earth of the home note, always stepping on clouds, from beginning to end, from life on earth to eternity beyond.

The four acids that make up DNA – adenine, guanine, cytosine and thymine, the building blocks of life – are mirrored by the four voices, soprano, alto, tenor and bass, the building blocks of music. And those building blocks of music split and split again as the music progresses; the choir breathes in and breathes out, and new life is formed within the notes themselves. There is no beginning and no end, just sound and beauty. And love.

I have never been baptised, christened, blessed in any religious way, but during that ferry journey down the Brisbane River, I felt a sacrament descend on me. Lauridsen, an American composer with the sound of the world in his ears, had blessed me with his song.

A sacrament of music.

To live a musician's life is to live a blessed life. Doris Lessing talks about the ether-reality of artists and musicians, being able to hover a little over the world, a perspective apart. My friend Lizzie once said how sorry she felt for people who didn't have music in their life. 'What do they have in their heads if it isn't a tune?'

Many years ago, I was playing a quartet gig for a party at a fancy Melbourne men's club. We were playing background music so we were mostly ignored, but we did get to practise pieces for a concert we had coming up. At the end people smiled politely and let us know, very nicely, that when we left, we could use the servants' exit. So very polite.

We exited through the main members' door (natch) and went to the McDonald's up the street. Even though we had just been paid, we were still young and broke, so McDonald's seemed a sensible option. It was the middle of another rudely long Melbourne winter, and we stood around in our big coats and delicate concert shoes, waiting for our order. An older woman approached us, so gently, a pianissimo entry.

'Excuse me, is this your cello?' She spoke in an Eastern European accent of wars and sonatas.

'Yes, it is. We just played next door. They kicked us out the servants' exit. Just like Mozart!'

She looked down at the floor, then past me, to another life.

'I wanted to play the cello when I was young. My father, he did not let me.'

My hands rested on the top of my cello case, calluses thick on the left hand, the right hand supple and blood-filled from an hour of playing. As the woman gazed at my hands, I drew them down into my pockets, embarrassed, guilty. My working hands were a sign of exceptional privilege, that I had music running through my veins, through my mind, every moment of my day, and I could pick up my cello and play Bach alone, or play Mozart with three others, and music kept my mind still and music shone a beam into the darkness.

I had been given that by my mother, and the woman from Eastern Europe had been denied it.

Most nights I talk with my mother by telephone in England, in a desperate bid to thank her for giving me music. For not allowing me to give up, and for reminding me to practise every single evening after her long, drab days working in a provincial civil service office. Since her stroke in 2017, Mum has continued to live on her own, with the care of my big sister

Liz and her family, and the NHS. The only bit of Mum that didn't fully recover after her stroke was her legs, but, as she says herself, she was never much of a walker. She was always more interested in her brain, which is back to doing cryptic crosswords. We talk about the weather (of course, we are English), I tell Mum about my students, my horn playing, how much I love Anna, her namesake, what Charlie is doing and how pretty Happy the Dog is. As the months go by since I've seen Mum, an urgency takes over me to say everything I need to say, to not leave anything out. To not have Mum die with something left ungiven, unthanked. It's a nightly playing of a piece of music, wanting to express everything written on the page and everything that isn't.

As we get older, a desperation can take over us to not leave anything out, to not leave anything undone or unexplored, to leave no room for what might have been but to make space for what can be. Will we choose to play music or not? If you do this, if you choose music, you can do anything. And you'll simply feel better about yourself. Few people can honestly say that.

———————————

For many musicians, no matter how advanced they are with their music, there is a singular pleasure in simply playing their instrument. Just as Arvo Pärt does not pay attention to how his music is played, so these musicians do not care whether they are playing Bach, Górecki or Sculthorpe. These musicians have music running in their veins and they wrap their bodies and their spirits around their music tools. Whether it is young Artie with his *Two Grenadiers*, Cathy with her Bach sonata, or Belinda with her Elgar Concerto, they love their instrument and all it provides. In that instrument lies their past, present and future.

Belinda Manwaring, cello player and teacher extraordinaire: 'I suppose I must say, I just love the *sound* of the cello. My favourite pieces would be Bach's *Arioso*, Paradis' *Sicilienne*, the slow movement of the Rachmaninoff Sonata, Saint-Saëns' *The Swan*, the slow movement of the Elgar Concerto, those pieces where the depth of the sound comes through. But it's also the physicality of playing the instrument. I played the violin; I even played viola for a week, but I said no, that's not low enough.

'When I tried the cello, I said, "Now it's low enough."'

When you love your instrument as much as that, practice is barely work, it becomes play. Belinda already loved her cello when she was fourteen, but it was only after a mediocre exam, not a successful one, that she decided to play properly. She got up at 5 a.m. to play her scales and played cello for three hours after school. Every single day. She let her homework pile up until the weekend. How can you do this if it is not through love?

When you go to a concert and watch the musicians on stage with their instruments, you witness a love scene – the way the instruments are held, cradled, swaddled in the arms of the players, embracing their clarinet or guitar in their palms, enveloping their violin in their arms, touching their trumpet oh so lightly with their lips. It is all so unbearably tender. When a musician is playing truthfully, without ego, they only want to show you how much their music can be adored. An authentic musician plays from love.

———————————

Music is composed for so many different reasons – for adoration, for adulation, for worship, for money, for revolution, for death, for joy, for love. But what about Olivier Messiaen's *Quartet for the End of Time*? Here is music of mystery in the strangest form, combining philosophy and musical order from the West and the East. This is a defining piece of the twentieth century and yet its meaning will always be a beat beyond our grasp.

Messiaen was French, born in 1908, educated by some of the greats of the French Romantic school – Widor, Dupré, Dukas – and went on to become the monumental French musical voice of the century. In 1940 Messiaen was enlisted into the French army as a medical orderly and immediately captured at Verdun. He was imprisoned by the Nazis in a camp called Stalag VIII-A where he met three other musicians – a violinist, Jean Le Boulaire, a clarinettist, Henri Akoka, and a cellist, Étienne Pasquier. Much has been made, and possibly exaggerated, of the conditions at the camp, but for many of the prisoners it was relative luxury compared with the living and dying nightmares of Auschwitz and Treblinka. One of the German officers, Karl-Albert Brüll, an admirer of Messiaen's music, made sure Messiaen had an early work duty so he could practise his ornithology, brought him manuscript paper and pencils, and cleared out a hut so he could compose.

With this quartet, Messiaen brought together many of his beliefs – spiritual, societal and musical – and expounded them as clearly and as logically as a thesis of words. His wish, his statement, in the title refers to the Book of Revelation and the End Times, but it also refers to music. So much of music up to this point had been composed with strict guidelines – bars, or measures, which we spoke about earlier in the book, with each bar guarded by bar lines – and so time became a regular, predictable entity. With this quartet, Messiaen takes away the bar lines, and therefore the bars, and leaves only rhythm. An unpredictable, unknowable, unspeakable rhythm. The music becomes life itself.

The quartet was composed in 1940 and performed in the camp the following year, after months of rehearsal.

The night of the performance, mid-winter in eastern Poland; the prisoners, guards, even the sick of the camp, gather in a barracks hut in the icy evening and listen in complete silence to the eight parts of the *Quartet for the End of Time*. The blackness of their situation, their life, their camp, is suddenly illuminated by the advent of Messiaen's music – a musical painting of birds in their pre-dawn chorus. An awakening for all to hear.

As the music goes out and out into the universe, as it beckons you to look to the deep rather than the distance, you are taken lower, lower, lower, and then, you arrive. At the centre of the piece, *Louange à l'Eternité de Jésus*, or *Praise to the Eternity of Jesus*, your world stills and settles. Your heartbeat slows and the music sings in an endless line of song, without any beat, but with a rhythm that insists on life and death and truth. Time does not stop, but it stops moving. The usual depth of the cello is replaced by a lift onto the summit of its range, a powerful man singing his radiant, ecstatic song.

As Messiaen himself wrote: 'Jesus is considered here as the Word. A broad phrase, "infinitely slow", on the violoncello, magnifies with love and reverence the eternity of the Word, powerful and gentle ... "In the beginning was the Word, and the Word was with God, and the Word was God."'

———————————

I have been practising my horny high notes, and I couldn't be happier. I can hear Charlie outside in the hallway so I open the door and ask, rhetorically, how much she must have been enjoying them.

'Oh, I have been ... out in the garden.'

Setting aside this I'm sure unintended slight, my high notes have been sounding a bit better. Well, better is a word I try to avoid, so I'll venture on the word 'fruitier'. I admit to having stolen this from neighbour Greg, who said I was sounding fruitier and that he didn't want me to take it the wrong way, but he heard me practising the other day and couldn't quite believe it was me. Greg, it was. (Hastily hiding the Barry Tuckwell recording.)

Anyhoo, now I know I can play my Gs with more substance, I can relax and try some of Peter's more challenging wisdoms, like allowing my embouchure to be 'perilously soft inside the mouthpiece'. While writing this book, I'm imagining Peter becoming a famous horn poet in addition to the poet of the horn that he already is. His phrases vibrate through my life beyond the lessons, just as Peter recommends breathing beyond the horn. Before I started my lessons with him, I had no idea such a Brass Buddha existed.

I'm continuing with my grade four pieces and have decided to let Euridice have some rest in Hades while I take a trip to Albania via a little folk ditty called *Dy Lule Mbas Malit*, or, if your Albanian is a bit rusty, *Two Flowers Over the Mountain*.

I feel a tad safer in this piece: although it is set on a mountain and not in hell, the notes are more foothills than peaks and only go up to a D. But if there's not as much difficulty in pitch, it means there must be difficulty elsewhere (you've got to watch out for those wily examiners), and the challenge in the mountains, perhaps appropriately, is to breathe quickly and deeply, and make a beautiful singing phrase sound unique each time on its three hundred and ninety-one repetitions. I make up a story of two Albanian shepherds falling in love, *Brokeback Mountain*–style, and the narrative gives me the air to fly through the piece. Towards the end, though, I notice a strange sound, a slight yet persistent hiss. Weird. I check Anna's valves and crooks, give her a twirl and try once more. Again, *sssss*, a sleepy viper inside my brain. Then I realise – it is coming from my mouth! My embouchure, the embouchure I have been working on like a prize fighter for months and months and months – feeding it, wetting it, massaging it, keeping it relaxed and plumped and moisturised – yes, that embouchure, has developed an air discharge. Which, put like that, sounds distinctly unpleasant.

I want to immediately call an ambulance, go to the nearest hospital and demand to see a lip specialist. Realising this might be an overreaction, I look in the mirror as I play to see what I can spot, and there it is: one side of my mouth is bubbling air, a bicycle puncture in the rain. I burst into tears and sulk. And text Peter.

Code red emergency! My embouchure has broken!

Peter, true to his Buddha status, remains calm in the face of face-calamity, observes my leaky lips in my next lesson, examines an ancient scar from a bike accident when my lower teeth went an impressively long way into my upper lip, and proclaims the *sssss* not a problem. In fact, it happens occasionally to him when he is tired. I'm sure he's just saying that to make me feel better. He reminds me to follow the process and it will go away of its own accord.

Over the next few weeks, as my exam looms, I practise with the *sssss* from my leaky lips, a constant reminder of the inconstancy of the horn. As if I needed one. Then one day I realise, without having consciously done anything, it's vanished. Once again, the Brass Buddha was right. Om. I was trying out *Maria*, Bernstein's classic from *West Side Story*, and I realised that where the song moves into a beguine rhythm my *sssss* had decided to begone. I am left with other issues though: Maria's voice is meant to be 'the most beautiful sound I ever heard', but I cannot seem to create a sound anything more alluring than a snoring rhino; still, an improvement on the sexed-up rhino from months before. And the end goes up to a long, quiet F and E, the top of the stave and the top of my ability. Playing these notes after playing the whole piece is as challenging as climbing the Sydney Harbour Bridge after running an ultra-marathon around the city. You want to at least have a cup of tea and put your feet up before you give it a crack. I practise, I fail, I practise, I fail and there is only one thing left to do – trust in Peter and his process.

The weeks and then the days recede before my horn spectacular. I begin to panic-practise (a not at all valid practice method) my scales, particularly the chromatic ones, where you go through every semitone. And the pesky F sharp harmonic minor scale, which I feel should simply be banned from coming anywhere near a horn. I play my scales slowly, I play them glacially, I play them in my head without my horn, I even try playing them on my horn without my head and nothing seems to stick. I have a lesson with Peter and ask for help.

'What, help to practise?'

Embarrassing. He suggests using the music when I practise, and then visualise the music as I play from memory. It helps going up, but nothing can help me coming down. Then I'm in freefall, and I just hope the examiner doesn't ask for F sharp bloody minor.

Early one morning Charlie, Happy and I go for a quick walk around the block. Happy is running off the leash (my bad) through the grass when a car makes a sharp turn into a driveway. I sprint to save Happy but forget I am wearing clogs. Clogs and running rarely compute, especially to my feet, which slip out of said clogs, leaving me freefalling in the air with one thought. No, two thoughts. 'Do not break your wrists. Do not break your wrists. Do not break your wrists. Oh, and do not break your face.'

As I lie crumpled face down on the concrete, Happy, oblivious, wanders over to see if I've found something to eat. Or if I might be good to sniff then wee on. I check my wrists and teeth; all good, but when I get up it's clear I won't be running again for a while. I have ruptured a knee ligament. It looks like I'll be walking into my horn exam on crutches.

The concert space is lit by the greatest stage light of them all, the mid-morning sun, and the audience is gathering on picnic rugs on the grass by Brisbane's Ascot Park rotunda, rather than in the sticky stalls of a concert hall. It's nearly Christmas and today is concert practice day for Bardon Strings. This will be the first performance of what Anne Keenan hopes will be many in a Round the Rotundas Tour of southeast Queensland. The mood in the orchestra, as well as the temperature in the rotunda, is sizzling.

I've been playing all year with Bardon Strings and it has become the highlight of my week. During the second term of 2020 we couldn't gather to rehearse, but Charles, a very strong violinist and technical wizard, kept the players together in music and spirit by organising regular online meetings, encouraging us to record our separate parts for some of our pieces and him mixing them together. Once we could all

gather again in person, the change in the orchestra's sound was unmistakable. Even though we hadn't been playing together for months, the strength and confidence of the players had continued to develop. They had become unstoppable.

The beauty of Bardon Strings is how naturally its progress has unfolded. This is because Anne teaches from love. Her energy comes from such a pure, open-hearted centre that although she comes to the rehearsals with an objective in mind, essentially the rehearsal will still be productive and perfect no matter what happens. The communal practice comes from a centre of devotion and reminds me of the process of the horn that Peter has drilled into me so caringly. The way Anne has set up the rehearsals means that people want to come and take part fully in them, with open heart and mind. For Bardon Strings, the rehearsal is the process. Right from the start, Anne wanted people to produce something they could be proud of, and they do. They are.

The dress rehearsal is done and all we need do is wait for the weather forecast for the following Sunday. Brisbane rain and rotundas and string instruments are a challenging mix in the Queensland summer.

Anne sends an emergency email on Friday to say that, miracle of pre-Christmas miracles, she has found us a community hall to perform in if necessary. By the following Sunday, it's raining so much you can't see out of the car window, and the Brisbane River is flexing its muscles and threatening to flood once more. The rotunda is out. Washed out. When we meet at the community hall at 9 a.m. I'm half-expecting three wise men to turn up, and in their own way they do – Ian, Pieter and Ben, each bearing their cellos and ready for action.

The rest of the musicians arrive, drenched and ecstatic. We are finally giving a concert, a year after the last one. We arrange chairs and music stands around our focus point, the conductor's podium, and our shepherd, Anne, calmly and lovingly ensures everything is ready for us to perform.

The audience gathers, dripping rain onto the wooden floor, and children play with their toy animals to the side. The light is muted inside the old hall and the rain outside creates a murmuration of comfort. Anne turns to the audience and tells the story of the creation of Bardon Strings. And then we play.

The sound of a solitary violin rings out into the hall. Luke, the leader of the orchestra, plays the beginning of Jay Ungar's *Ashokan Farewell* and our minds are taken away from the rain of Brisbane and the approach of Christmas to a place of profound satisfaction at what we have, and a forgotten sorrow of what could never be. How can music give us such complexity with so few notes? Just as in *Quartet for the End of Time*, time stands still in this concert. It is forever playing, forever perfect.

Music is our shelter, our friend, our guide, our rebirth, our gift, to give and receive.

Anne beams throughout the concert. Just as Michel Brandt in Schubert's *Unfinished Symphony* hardly needed to conduct us, it is the same with Anne. Her presence is enough. She continues to beam after the concert. The performance of Bardon Strings could not have been more cohesive or convincing.

Anne's words say everything.

'My idea of putting people's wellbeing before a polished musical performance is right, because people blossom in that way. And I get a lot of satisfaction from having that approach.'

We celebrate after the concert with cake, and Anne looks fulfilled. Not only by the cake, but by her work with the orchestra.

'I wanted to find a way of living the rest of my life that was meaningful, I suppose. I didn't want to just feel I was going to work, feeling exhausted, burnt out. I wanted to spend some of my life giving something to other people. Yes, I'm giving something to other people, but they give me heaps! That's so good, to be able to do that. To find a way to meaningfully express yourself through your work.

'And music – I love it.'

_____

'Your job as the parent, and my job as the teacher, is to sprinkle stardust all around that child so it falls on them somewhere. That's where environment comes in. We need to make sure there's a warmth and a care and love in our mind before we play music with the child. We can create the environment where playing is a joy or, at least if they don't feel like it, it's never an unpleasant thing, and the child isn't punished or growled at or coerced.'

Kim Bishop is a violin teacher, originally from Melbourne but now based in Hobart. Kim is not any ordinary violin teacher – she is one of the most highly experienced Suzuki teachers and trainers in Australia. Kim studied the Suzuki method at university in the United States and returned to Australia, where she developed a studio in Melbourne full of violin students with the most extraordinary ability. This ability you may think came from 'talent', but its roots lie in the students' environment and their dedication to process. Their dedication to daily practice, which is itself planted in love.

Kim talks about the essence of environment in the development of a musician of any age. If a parent is negative or mocking about the child playing music, or shames the child if they feel they are not making a 'good' sound, or makes the child feel as if they are wasting their parents' money and time and, perhaps worst of all, their own time, then the child will constantly and profoundly, although not necessarily consciously, feel negatively towards playing music. The stardust sprinkled by parents and carers and teachers is an assurance that no matter what happens with the child and their music, they will be supported and loved.

When we are six, we are dependent on our carers to provide our environment, but as we grow we take more and more charge of the mood of our lives: we become parents to ourselves. But just like our parents could be towards us, we can often be negative towards ourselves. When we are learning something new, do we provide care and warmth and love? Are we patient with ourselves? Do we forgive our mistakes and return the next day with a renewed optimism? Do we ensure we love the process as much as the dream of the end? Do we give ourselves the best chance for success by playing our instruments with ease, joy and glory?

As teachers, we need to nurture the child within the student, no matter whether the student is six or fifty-six. And as parents to ourselves, we need to do the same. It can be so simple; Kim talks of a series of tiny successes.

'If you have a little success, you realise your potential. Dr Suzuki was really onto something by advocating producing one thing to a high level. It's a meditative way of looking at things, like making a beautiful sound on your A string. Once you find that deeper resonant sound, it becomes your own knowledge. Once you can attach that beautiful sound to your desire, you start to take flight.'

This knowledge and success becomes a feedback loop of feeling – through our fingertips, the tingle as you know you're playing in tune, or the groove of the bow as you know it's just the right speed and angle and weight to pull a deep sound from your instrument. This success shows us knowledge on many different levels, levels that can go beyond any cognitive understanding. This knowledge combines physical and intellectual confidence, proprioceptive experience, abstract and spiritual awareness, and, perhaps most meaningful of all, the appreciation that there is always more to find, and always more to give. How can it get any better than this?

'We are all musical. Music not only helps us with sensitivity and character development, respect for others, recognition of beauty, but music can also be very intimate. It's something we can have on our own, regardless of what social experience we have had. I don't know many musicians who haven't taken their instrument out alone and not wanted anyone to come into the room while they're playing. Anyone can take that quiet time on their own and have their music express themselves and find that point where they produce something they love, something which is part of them. If you didn't have that nurturing upbringing, you'll either never have it or you'll have to find it for yourself. *You* have to look for it.'

Just as Kim says, if you haven't been given love in your life, music can give you the space to find it within yourself. No matter your age or your ability. The potential is always there, you need only sprinkle your own stardust.

The day has come. It's been nearly a year since I walked into Peter Luff's studio and began horn lessons with him. Over that year I have fallen in love with the horn, and along the way have learnt a considerable amount about myself. I have learnt I am stubborn, driven, persistent, selfish, and that I will practise and practise if I want to achieve something. And now the first big challenge of my horn odyssey is here. Slightly complicated by needing to go into the exam room on crutches. I decide I am going to man up (title of my next book), ditch the crutches and stand to play my exam. Hopefully, my knee will last through *Maria* and make it down the Albanian mountainside.

I have been rehearsing with Helen Devane, a magnificent pianist who taught me piano for a while; unfortunately, the piano didn't stick for me but our friendship did, and Helen's playing disguises the occasional accidents in my own. The day before the exam, I have had a mock exam with Peter via Zoom from Melbourne. Peter has been teaching elite brass players at the Australian National Academy of Music all week, and I am amazed he finds the time to put me through my paces. I am happy with how I play (apart from those enigmatic scales), but Peter says something brilliantly apt. He seems to have a talent for that.

'Ed, play within your limits. You are trying to make phrases above your current technical ability, you're wanting to do things you're not quite ready to do, so you're compromising the sound. You've got to play where you can sit comfortably. Don't play too fast, don't use too much rubato. Sit inside the middle of the note.'

I realise my ego has been pushing me to places I am not ready to go, and the Brass Buddha has saved me. Once again.

Charlie and Happy drive me to the exam centre, kiss me good luck (well, Happy's is more of a sniff and a lick), and Helen and I go to our warm-up room. A small girl pops her head in to ask if she can collect her trumpet case. I ask how her exam went and which grade, and she replies her grade four went very well.

'How old are you?'

'I'm eleven.'

Aha. That's why her trumpet comes up to her waist. I mention I am doing the same grade at fifty-four, and she looks slightly sorry for me.

'I'm sure you'll be fine ...'

A lovely woman with a clipboard comes in and invites me to go to the exam room. There, behind a desk covered in papers, stands a smiling man with the kindest face you could wish for in an examiner.

'So, Eadric, make yourself comfortable. Let's start with *Che Farò Senza Euridice?*.'

As Helen plays the introduction, a chord of horn memories peals through my mind: Peter and his wisdoms, his patience and kindness and humour but above all his love for this instrument; Charlie and her limitless encouragement, and her ability to meditate even through my horn exercises; my neighbours, most of whom have stayed (except next door who moved several suburbs away just to be on the safe side); my mum, who gave me not just this instrument but my complete world of music. And finally I think of the simplicity of music and playing like a child again, without ego and within my limits, playing like Artie, playing for the sheer love of it.

In my arms I cradle Anna, my horn, my new friend, a companion on the greatest journey of them all, the journey into yourself. The introduction to Euridice comes to an end and it is time for my first note. I lift my horn to my lips, breathe in and step into the middle of the note, into the sound, into the music. The horn gives its call, and all I need do is follow.

I receive an A+.

It is Saturday morning and I am sitting in a cello lesson with Edwina, the teacher of children with additional needs who holds curiosity as a central tenet in her life. I've just asked how her mum is, as she has recently been diagnosed with dementia.

'One of the things that Mum always remembers is the cello lesson. Mum always asks, "How is the cello?" That gives me a great deal of pleasure because it's still a connection I have with Mum when there's a great loss of other things. But that's one thing she remembers, so we can maintain that connection, because it's still in reality. So much of what Mum talks about is in the past, or has not actually happened, so that gives me a great deal of joy.'

Edwina was forty-seven when she decided to learn the cello. Over the last three years she has dedicated herself to practice – daily, repetitive, attentive practice. After two years playing on an abandoned school cello, Edwina bought her own instrument, a perfect three-quarter size for her smaller hands. She sits with it now, her left hand casually resting on the cello's shoulder, her bow hand relaxed, holding the bow so lightly it falls beyond her knee. Edwina says she doesn't even think about her bow hold now – it's as familiar as picking up a pencil. I reply that she doesn't need to think about it, as it is very good, unlike some of my younger students who I wish would do a little more bow-hold thinking. Ho hum.

Edwina lets her legs fall around her cello, and she begins to play. A slow scale coming down, to warm up: do (a deer) followed by ti (for two) rather than a re (of sun). Playing scales from the top down allows the left hand to settle and the fingers to be in place, an orderly line of schoolchildren waiting for lunch. It's reassuring, coming down. Edwina's sound is amber and refined, a true reflection of her character. Her bow moves over the strings, going deeper and slower the lower she goes. Her face is determined and focused and exquisitely calm; nothing in the music is missed, nothing is untended, everything is loved in Edwina's cello garden.

Edwina is naturally self-conscious and has had to work on managing those intrinsic stresses throughout her life. Through learning meditation, Edwina is finding it easier to let go of feeling self-conscious in all aspects, including her cello. Playing cello when you know someone is listening is not easy, with anxiety waiting in your lap.

'I've noticed I'm not thinking when I'm playing cello; my head is full, so I can't think about anything else. I feel I'm quite hyper-focused.'

Mindfulness in life, mindfulness in cello. Mindfulness in cello, mindfulness in life.

I ask Edwina how she feels now about choosing to learn the cello.

'It's one of the best decisions in my life. I would say I was meant to do it; it was meant to happen. I feel that if I did give it up, I would be losing so much. More than the instrument. I would be losing so much enjoyment, so much knowledge; it would be a real tragedy if I gave it up. I know it's going to be a challenge, but there will come a time … a friend who is a musician has said to me, "It will come, just give it time. Give it time, give it time."'

I point out to Edwina that the pieces she was playing a year ago she can now play very easily, and the pieces she is learning now will be easy for her in a year's time.

'All natural things are coming,' as my friend Cami would say.

Edwina nods and says there have been moments when she has played and she doesn't remember anything, but the music just plays through her body. The music is sinking down into a deeper part of her consciousness.

'And I look at my fingers and I see now I have calluses on my fingertips and they look like a musician's, and isn't that great? Because I feel like a musician.'

Playing the cello has not only improved Edwina's relationship with herself, it has helped in her relationship with her mother.

After Edwina had been learning for about a year, she brought her mother along to a lesson, the one she has never forgotten. Edwina's mother, June, is in her late eighties. Alert, serene and beautifully dressed in white, June sat on a chair a little to the side. She had never seen Edwina play the cello before and I could feel the amazement, the awe, the respect as she gazed at her daughter. At the end of the lesson, June hugged me and thanked me for teaching Edwina. It felt like the gratitude of the poet Massoud Khalili in Afghanistan, who had watched me teach Besheda, a refugee. The size of June's gratitude was overwhelming.

For Edwina, playing the cello has also changed her in other people's eyes. 'When I tell people I play the cello, it's as if I've said I've just won the Nobel Peace Prize. And I'm going, "No, no, lower your expectations!" So many people say to me, "I really wish I'd kept that up as a child, I really wish I could do that, I should go back to learning the viola, the violin, the clarinet, oh wow, how do you do that?" Well, I just go and have lessons. It's not rocket science. People think you have to be a particular type of person, with a particular brain or experience or come from a musical background.'

There is no such thing as talent, there is only love. Love for what you are learning, and therefore a desire to know it more deeply, more comprehensively, to have that knowledge become a part of you, and you of it. Love creates the passion, and the passion creates the energy to work. The spark of love takes time, but it does come. The teacher's role is to keep their students playing until that spark happens, and when it does, the students take off and mostly teach themselves. From me pushing and pulling them onwards, they become an upright rolling wheel, the teacher just brushing the wheel forward, not too hard, not too often, not disturbing the natural momentum. It takes some wisdom to know when and where to push your students, and such love to stand aside and let them move ahead, knowing you may never see them again. To teach music, to teach anything, requires our hearts to be open and ready for everything, never expecting, always hoping. Always hoping the love will grow and the choice is made.

Playing music is a choice we may not make initially as a child but we can certainly make as adults. Listening, properly listening to music is a choice we can make at any age. And it is choosing to play music, and choosing to properly listen to ourselves and others, that brings us to the highest escarpment of all: love. Edwina shows us how. Edwina perseveres with her playing with such strength and joy, she is unstoppable.

'Music is a gift that can be given at any age. It can be someone who has given you that gift through your family, or it's a gift you can give yourself. And it's recognising you're worthy of that gift. Because a lot of people don't think they are worthy of it.

'But I am.'

Yes. You are.

The music room at school is packed with open viola and cello cases, and young and old musicians preparing their instruments. I am standing in the middle, trying to direct traffic, tune instruments, rosin bows, find lost music, chat with parents, replace frayed strings, and encourage the more timid of my students that they have done the work, they will not melt or freeze on stage, they need only trust in the music.

It's concert day.

I admit, as a teacher I probably get more nervous than my students in their concerts. I continually second-guess myself: did I concentrate enough on phrasing? Do they have a lovely bow hold? Are they comfortable when they play? Did we do enough performance practice? And, most importantly of all, will they enjoy themselves?

Parents and siblings are slowly exiled to the concert space next door and my students and I make our final preparations.

Many musicians see playing a concert, performing, as the benediction of all our work. When we perform, the addition of an audience and a small (or large) amount of stress induces deeper and wider emotions, more attention to sound, a feeling of the music stretching beyond reality to what might be. Just as the Schubert *Unfinished Symphony* in the Alps went beyond anything we had given before, that sentiment can be accessed at any stage in our learning. We only need to practise.

I remind my students that we are here to share our music with the people we love. And if they feel nervous, to know that nerves and excitement are the same thing, and it is a good thing to be so excited about playing the instrument they love. And to keep singing their song. They have fulfilled their process and now is the time to share their music with others.

And we go out on stage.

Rosie begins the concert. She has chosen to wear a simple blue dress and takes her seat with a slight nod to the audience. I observe her with awe; she has such poise at the age now of eight. Although we have done a significant amount of concert preparation, the only true way to prepare for a concert is to play a concert, so as a teacher I can never be completely sure how my students will react to a big audience. Rosie introduces her piece, *French Folk Song*, to the crowd and makes herself comfortable with her cello snuggling next to her heart, her bow nestled in soft fingers. I start the accompaniment with a light waterfall of notes; Rosie looks at me, smiles a knowing smile, and plays.

It is perfect. From her first note to her last, Rosie's debut performance is flawlessly representative of the work she has done all year. The assuredness of her playing, her glorious sound, the flow of her phrasing – all of it is because Rosie has followed the process and, through that, has fallen in love with the cello.

And through her love for the cello, Rosie now knows, in her heart, her mind and her body, many things.

She knows that hearing is different from listening. She knows that her mind and body are one, and what we think we can do is what we end up being able to do.

She knows persistence. She knows that tiny steps, taken each day, create a journey unimaginable in length and adventure. She knows that it is alright not to be able to do something. But then, note by note, she is succeeding.

She knows how to express emotions rather than keep them inside where they can twist and warp us.

She knows the kindness of music, especially when we play music with and for others.

She knows just how much you can do, even when you are eight years old.

Rosie knows not only how to learn but why we learn.

And Rosie knows that music will always be there. She knows that from today until the end of her life, she will never be alone.

THE MOHAN VEENA is a hybrid of instruments from the West and the East: a regular acoustic guitar is modified with melody strings, additional sympathetically vibrating strings and drone strings, played with a plectrum or mizrab, and, to change the pitch of the notes, a glass ball is slid up and down the strings, which are treated with coconut oil. The resulting sound is one of endless vibration, the notes blooming and multiplying, creating a garden of harmony.

This instrument, and the less chimerical slide guitar, are used on an album by two musicians who only met an hour before the album was recorded. The musicians are Ry Cooder and Vishwa Mohan Bhatt, and the album is *A Meeting by the River*.

Sometimes in our lives we hear music that we know will become our dear friend. The sympathetic vibrations of the music sing out into the world and pull you into their sphere, sinking deeper and deeper into you as the years go on. One of those pieces for me is this album, specifically, the final track, *Isa Lei*.

I was introduced to this music by Ivan Lloyd, who for many years was the master music programmer on ABC Classic. Ivan has that almost unteachable gift of choosing the exact music for the moment, and one morning he presented me with this.

Years ago, when I first heard *A Meeting by the River*, I was beginning to descend into the profound depression that would lead to me losing everything then: my job, my partner, my house, my purpose. As I descended into depression, I had stopped playing music for myself and only listened to music in my job on the radio. Symphonies and sonatas and concertos would play in the studio as I presented a music show, but nothing sunk in. Except this.

Ry Cooder, with his seminal sound of loneliness in film soundtracks like *Paris, Texas*, begins the simple song, taking us to an isle of contentment. He and Vishwa Mohan Bhatt play in the kindest harmony, blending their lines in an embrace of selfless love. All the way through the music a pattern of notes falls, always relaxing and always supporting, a hand beneath the music, cradling the players with sweet devotion.

I would listen to this music in my depression, but slowly even this piece became dulled to me and eventually meant nothing. Like a window inexorably misting over, I couldn't see through my depression to feel anything or hear anything. All these years later, I listen to the same music and am overwhelmed with happiness. True, I lost everything. But I lost it all to be ready to receive what was waiting for me all along. Myself.

The only truth is music.

JACK KEROUAC

To GIVE OURSELVES MUSIC is a gift at the most profound level. To play music gives us a fresh start, an agency over ourselves and a connection with ourselves. With music, we let go of self-hatred and move towards self-acceptance. It is a simple question: how can we hate ourselves when we are playing music?

We are all reborn every day through music, whether we are playing or listening or remembering. Remembering the times we listened to Grieg with our grandmother, or Chopin with our mother, or mourning the times we never had to listen with our father. We all have music running through our veins. Can you feel it?

We can be like Cathy with her dreams of playing Bach, or Jim with his persistence and bush music, or Benjamin with his eternal search for where the music lies, or Belinda with her simple love of playing, or Claudia and her discovery of her confidence, or Edwina with her gift to herself, or Liam and his dedication to classical music alone, or young Artie and his ecstasy of playing, or Rosie and her excitement at the sheer adventure of it all, or Megan, making her notes whole.

Let music into your life. Let process and practice and play come in. Let the magnificence of music enter you, and don't be afraid. Let music guide you to bravery, knowledge, resilience, kindness, wisdom, hope and love.

Music is the illumination of our lives, and music is humanity's greatest creation. Playing it and listening to it binds us in a mystery. And you, in these ecstatic days of your life, will be glad, so glad, that you became part of that mystery.

This has been a book of words. I hope some inspiring, powerful, provocative words. But words can only go so far. Music, the best music, begins where words end. It is time to play your part.

CODA

THIS IS THE MOMENT, when the music ends. A moment of deepest silence – between breath, between thought, between sound itself.

The musician, instrument in hand, stands on stage and takes their bow.

They bow to you, for coming to listen.

They bow to themselves, for their dedication to their art.

They bow to the musicians who have come before them and kept this art alive.

But above all, they bow to music itself.

This ritual is at the end of every concert, no matter the skill of the performer, the age of the performer, the type of music or where the music is played. This ritual is our step beyond beauty.

Because music consoles and restores us. Through music, whether we are listening or playing, we know ourselves more intimately, more honestly, and more clearly with every note. And with every note, music offers us a hand to the beyond.

Through music, we can say what we didn't even know we felt.

This book is an ode to music and a celebration of humanity's greatest creation. And this book is not a call to arms but a call to instruments.

Music offers us gifts we can open every day to make our lives whole, so let the playing begin.

THE MUSIC

BRAVERY

Maria Theresa von Paradis – *Sicilienne*

Frédéric Chopin – *Nocturne* in E-flat major

Richard Strauss – *A Hero's Life*

Pyotr Tchaikovsky – Symphony No. 5 (slow movement)

Sergei Rachmaninoff – Piano Concerto No. 2

Edward Elgar – Cello Concerto

Pandit Ravi Shankar – anything

Stéphane Grappelli – everything

Kathryn Griesinger – *Ring of Fire*

Jean-Jacques Rousseau – *Go Tell Aunt Rhody*

Arvo Pärt – *Spiegel im Spiegel*

KNOWLEDGE

Igor Stravinsky – *The Rite of Spring*

Joaquín Rodrigo – *Concierto de Aranjuez*

Anton Horner – *60 Studies*

Richard Wagner – *Siegfried's Funeral March*

John Tavener – *The Lamb*

Keith Sharp – *Campfire Glow*

Edvard Grieg – Piano Concerto

J.S. Bach – Cello Suite No. 3

Elton John – *Candle in the Wind*

Shinichi Suzuki – *Perpetual Motion*

RESILIENCE

Dimitri Shostakovich – Viola Sonata

Ludwig van Beethoven – *Moonlight Sonata*

Georg Telemann – Viola Concerto

Twinkle, Twinkle, Little Star

Pyotr Tchaikovsky – Violin Concerto

Antonio Vivaldi – *The Four Seasons*

Thomas de Hartmann and George Gurdjieff –
   folk music arrangements

Peter Sculthorpe – *Little Passacaglia*

Henryk Górecki – String Quartet No. 3 *Songs Are Sung* and
   Symphony No. 3 *Symphony of Sorrowful Songs*

Pablo de Sarasate – *Gypsy Airs*

J.S. Bach – Sonata No. 1 in G major (for viola da gamba)

KINDNESS

Matthew Hindson – *The Stars Above Us All*

Max Richter – *Mercy*

Traditional – *Stew Pot Hop*

Galina Grigorjeva – *In Paradisum*

Henry Purcell – *When I Am Laid in Earth*

Antonín Dvořák – Symphony No. 6

Béla Bartók – Viola Concerto

WISDOM

Michael Tippett – String Quartet No. 2

Christoph Willibald Gluck – *Che Farò Senza Euridice?*

Edward Elgar – Cello Concerto, Symphony No. 1
   and Violin Concerto

Zoltán Kodály – Adagio

J.S. Bach – Cello Suite No. 2

Franz Schubert – *Unfinished Symphony*

François-Joseph Gossec – *Gavotte*

James Horner – *My Heart Will Go On* (theme from *Titanic*)

HOPE

Robert Schumann – *The Happy Farmer* and
   The Two Grenadiers

J.S. Bach – Sonata No. 3 in G minor
   (for viola da gamba and keyboard)

Anon. – *French Folk Song*

Camille Saint-Saëns – *Romance* in F major

Pyotr Tchaikovsky – *Chanson Triste*

Cyril Tawney – *Grey Funnel Line*

LOVE

Morten Lauridsen – *O Magnum Mysterium*

J.S. Bach – *Arioso*

Maria Theresia von Paradis – *Sicilienne*

Sergei Rachmaninoff – Cello Sonata (slow movement)

Camille Saint-Saëns – *The Swan*

Olivier Messiaen – *Quartet for the End of Time*

Anon., Albania – *Dy Lule Mbas Malit*

Jay Ungar – *Ashokan Farewell*

Leonard Bernstein – *Maria*

Ry Cooder and Vishwa Mohan Bhatt – *A Meeting by the River*

A SHORT
GUIDE TO
LISTENING

Musical training is a more
potent instrument
than any other, because
rhythm and harmony
find their way into the
inward places of the soul.

PLATO, *THE REPUBLIC*

But I don't know anything
about classical music.
That's why I don't listen to it.

SUE, THE REPUBLIC HOTEL

PEOPLE OFTEN DECLARE they want to know more about classical music, so they can enjoy it.

'But why?' I ask. 'I don't know a single thing about pop music, or jazz, or funk, but I just like listening to it anyway. I don't know the name of the songwriters or who played bass or what year it was written. Crikey, I don't even listen to the lyrics. I just like the music. Can you just listen to classical music for, you know, the music?'

'Sure,' they reply, looking doubtful. 'But where do I start? It was okay when you could go to a record shop and browse, but nowadays it's all online and the app learns your preferences and just keeps playing you what you know already. It's hard to find something new.'

Aha. Now we're getting somewhere. Where do we start so we can find something new?

In this section I aim to tell you enough about classical music that when you go to a music app, you will be able to choose what music to listen to for yourself. Apps always send you to Mozart, and sure, he's great for weddings and funerals, but what about the bits in between?

Classical music is not a mystery. It is not a secret cult. It is not exclusive. I believe that if you can follow a recipe, you can develop an excellent knowledge of classical music.

The easiest way to listen to classical music is to first remove the name 'classical'. It's just music. Sure, sometimes it's old, sometimes it's long, but it uses the same twelve notes and the same rhythms as any other type of Western music.

It can be useful to arrange music into different parts of the day. Now, assuming you like things to be straightforward when you wake up and you don't like anything too shrill, I would recommend that you: a) stay away from sopranos or tenors for an hour or two; and b) try out composers like Debussy (*Rêverie, Arabesques, Clair de Lune*), Max Richter (his version of *The Four Seasons*), anything played on the viola da gamba, and Handel and Corelli. Their concerti grossi will wake you up with just the right amount of stimulation that means you won't be in a grump by the time you eat breakfast. If things are really looking stressful for the day, go with Gregorian chant. You'll feel like you've meditated for five hours after just five minutes.

When you're on the way to work, maybe in a traffic jam, maybe on a packed bus, you need calm but you also need concentration. This is where Schubert (his early symphonies (especially No. 5), Philip Glass (piano music, but it must be played by Sally Whitwell) and J.S. Bach really come into their own. Bach's music, especially the Brandenburg Concertos, has such an inevitable flow and logic to it you will be flowing into the workplace yourself. And wondering how anyone could be listening to anything else.

It's time to get down to work, in the office, in the garden, volunteering. You might prefer silence for a few hours (there's even a piece for that – John Cage's *4'33"*; you can buy it on iTunes for $1.69), or you might like some trotting-along music – Elena Kats-Chernin and her *Re-Inventions*, Mendelssohn's *Songs Without Words*, Terry Riley and his comforting, repetitive *In C*, Wim Mertens' *Close Cover*, Milhaud's *Le Boeuf sur le Toit* or Prokofiev and the ballet music for *Romeo and Juliet*.

By lunchtime you'll be ready for, well, lunch, but also for something a tad chewier than soup. This is the time to get stuck into something chunky – a Beethoven piano concerto, something Russian like Glazunov's Symphony No. 2 or Shostakovich Quartet No. 3, anything by Anna Pavlova (to match your dessert) and maybe a Sculthorpe quartet, especially No. 14 *Quamby*.

As the afternoon stretches over the horizon, there are so many directions to go. You could continue down the muscular line with more big symphonies by Mahler or Bruckner, you could delve into the world of small groups with piano trios by Ross Edwards or Clara Schumann, take a trip to South Africa and Kevin Volans' *Hunting: Gathering*, visit a whole new sound world with Toru Takemitsu and his *Rain Coming*, or music from South America with Heitor Villa-Lobos and Alberto Ginastera.

As the afternoon folds into early evening, on your way home it's an opportunity to give your mind a salve – *Four Estonian Lullabies* by Veljo Tormis, John Tavener and his *Protecting Veil*, Simeon ten Holt's *Palimpsest*, anything by Anouar Brahem. This is music to soothe, to massage, to hush.

In the evening, as the light darkens and your world folds into itself, you can really venture along psychological paths – Schoenberg and his *Transfigured Night*, Beethoven's final Quartet No. 16, or opera with Alban Berg's *Lulu*, Bartók's *Bluebeard's Castle*, Strauss's *Salome*. Nothing on TV will come close to the suspense of this music. But before you go to bed, perhaps it's good to end where we started – some Gregorian chant, Max Richter's *On the Nature of Daylight*, and, to end your day, a Bach chorale.

And tomorrow, you can wait and hear what the world has to offer you. Music, good music, is an endless gift to yourself.

WITH THANKS

Thank you to HarperCollins Publishers, especially Mary Rennie. Mary, you came to me with the idea for this book, and I couldn't have written it without your support. Or without the brilliant, sympathetic editing of Simone Ford. You are both a delight to work with. Thanks also to Barbara McClenahan for bringing everything together.

Thank you to my Brass Buddha, Peter Luff. Peter, you have given me lessons in so much more than the horn, and every one of your students is so fortunate to have you as their teacher. Your horn poetry stretches beyond music. I hope I can continue to have many more lessons with you.

Thank you to Richard Smart for suggesting I write a book all those years ago. Four books later and Richard, I think you were onto something.

Thank you to Martin Buzacott for keeping me going, talking me through my blocks, for saying, 'You've got this.' And for distracting me with bicycles.

Thank you to my cello teacher extraordinaire, Belinda Manwaring. Belinda, I look forward to finally doing enough practice for you.

Thank you to Dr Gale Bearman, Dr Leonie Todhunter, Dr Alys Saylor and Eliane Mathiuet for looking after my hormones, my knees, my chest and my mind.

Thank you to Dr Catherine Crock. Your shining example of kindness in medicine is life-changing for so many.

Thank you to all my students. I wish I could teach you as much as you teach me.

Thank you to Anne Keenan and all the musicians at Bardon Strings. Your joy in music is inspirational.

Thank you to Sophie Maxwell for saying all those years ago that I might be interested in becoming a Suzuki teacher. Sophie, how did you know before I did?

Thank you to Tina Brain, galvaniser, font of horn knowledge and a pillar of horn teaching in Australia.

Thank you to all the musicians and teachers I interviewed for this book. Your work is the most important.

Thank you to my neighbours, especially Greg and Erika. How long do you think the new neighbours will last?

Thank you to the Pattersons, my Australian family. Thank you for listening to my horn playing and smiling and applauding, even in its very early stages when others might have, actually I think some did, run from the room.

Thank you to my mum, Anna. For music, for everything.

And finally, thank you to Charlie. My lioness, my sun, and now my wife. I love you.

REFERENCES FOR QUOTATIONS

ix: Rumi, 13th-century Persian poet.

6: Leonard Bernstein, *Findings*, Simon & Schuster, New York, 1982.

64: William Blake, 'The Lamb', *Songs of Innocence*, London, 1789.

88: T.S. Eliot, 'The Dry Salvages', the third of the 'Four Quartets',
Faber and Faber Ltd, London, 1941. Reprinted with permission.

92: Dr Shinichi Suzuki, *Ability Development From Age Zero*, Alfred
Publishing Company, USA, 1999.

115: Jane Taylor, 'The Star', *Rhymes for the Nursery*, Darton and Harvey,
London, 1806.

123: Velimir Khlebnikov, 'When Horses Die', *Collected Works, Volume 3 –
Selected Poems*, Harvard University Press, Cambridge, MA, 1998.

125: Eddie Ayres, *Danger Music*, Allen & Unwin, Sydney, 2017.

138: Matt Haig, *How to Stop Time*, Penguin Books, New York, 2019.

176: Johann Wolfgang von Goethe, *Zahme Xenien*, Germany, 1796.

180: Charlie Parker, from Nat Shapiro and Nat Hentoff's *Hear Me
Talkin' to Ya: The Story of Jazz by Men Who Made It*, Rinehart,
New York, 1955.

189: Hermann Hesse, *Siddhartha*, New Directions Publishing, New York,
1922.

202: Arvo Pärt, from the original score of *Spiegel im Spiegel*, Universal
Edition, 1977.

205: Salman Rushdie, *Midnight's Children*, Jonathan Cape, London, 1981.

212: Arthur O'Shaughnessy, 'Ode', *Music and Moonlight Poems and
Songs*, Chatto and Windus, London, 1873.

220: Robert Schumann, 19th-century German composer.

248: Cyril Tawney, 'Grey Funnel Line', 1959.

250: Michael Leunig, 'Let it go, Let it out', 1992. Reprinted with permission.

261: Olivier Messiaen, notes translated from score by Anthony Gilbert.

261: John 1:1, *World English Bible*, Project Gutenberg, 2005.

284: Jack Kerouac, *Desolation Angels*, Deutsch, London, 1960.

298: Plato, *The Republic*, circa 375 BC.